Praise for *Managing the Gray Areas*:

"When Jerry Manas writes on leadership, I pay attention. *Managing the Gray Areas* is his best work yet and will open up a new path for leaders."
> – Pat Williams, Senior Vice President, Orlando Magic, and Author of *Souls of Steel*

"Jerry Manas systematically and vividly exposes the fallacies of outmoded black and white thinking and decision-making approaches. In this paradigm-shifting and eye-opening book, Jerry introduces a new, powerful, and compelling set of practices and tools, which leaders of teams, organizations, and even nations can apply to motivate their constituencies and better navigate the ambiguities of today's complex business environment. A standing ovation!"
> – Doug DeCarlo, Author of *eXtreme Project Management: Using Leadership, Principles and Tools for Delivering Value in the Face of Volatility*

"*Managing the Gray Areas* is an excellent book for every aspiring leader, offering great insights into principle-based leadership and decision making.
> – Scott Raskin, CEO, Mindjet

"There is no escaping the complexity of decision making in an increasingly gray world, whether in business or in life. Jerry Manas' *Managing the Gray Areas* is a thoughtful and highly useful exploration of the key issues every leader should consider when facing this reality."
> – Anthony Ibargüen, CEO, Alliance Consulting Group

"Manas provides the perfect examples to complement the guidelines, techniques, and tools this book offers. *Managing the Gray Areas* is a must-read for anyone wishing to improve or develop their leadership skills and enhance organizational results."
> – Matthew T. Sheaff, Senior Director, The Performance Institute

"In *Managing the Gray Areas,* Jerry Manas reveals how to tackle the thorny issues inherent in business when dealing with complex challenges and decision making. Leaders today need a mirror to see their blindspots, and the wisdom distilled in this landmark book can provide that mirror. Whether explaining concepts such as "blameless feedback" or balancing structure and flexibility, this book will surprise and inspire even the most seasoned and veteran business leaders."

    – Todd Colbeck, MBA, President, Colbeck Coaching Group

"In today's constantly changing and turbo-charged work environment, managers are regularly challenged to address a myriad of ethical questions that have no clear-cut answers. In *Managing the Gray Areas,* Jerry Manas provides sage advice on navigating through dilemmas by tackling issues through a holistic, systems approach. He has synthesized lessons from thought leaders in different disciplines, and offers refreshing guidance on leading with compassion and integrity while still focusing on organizational objectives. This is a must-read!"

    – Cindy Joy Marselis, Management Information Systems Professor, Fox School of Business and Management, Temple University

Managing the Gray Areas

Essential Insights for Leading People,
Projects & Organizations

Premier Edition

By Jerry Manas

To Sharon and Elizabeth—
Again and always.

Managing the Gray Areas: Essential Insights for Leading People,
Projects & Organizations, Premier Edition by Jerry Manas

Printed in the United States of America

ISBN: 978-1-932735-11-6
Library of Congress Control Number: 2007942245

RMC Publications, Inc.
Phone: 952.846.4484
Fax: 952.846.4844
E-mail: info@rmcpublications.com
Web: www.rmcpublications.com

Table of Contents

A special Web site (www.rmcpublications.com/grayareas) has been created specifically for readers of this book. I encourage you to use it to download and print selected graphics and tables from this book to reference as you apply the principles discussed in the following chapters. I will add occasional updates to the content, including new tools and ideas for gray area thinking. The site also includes a discussion forum, giving readers the opportunity to share thoughts, comments, and questions with other readers of this book. You will see a reminder to access the discussion forum at the end of each chapter. Use this opportunity to learn by dialoguing with other leaders as we navigate the gray areas together.

Foreword

Jerry Manas takes on reality and complexity. He takes on conflict and its underlying roots. He has a curiosity and a rigor; he has a depth of knowledge and a focus. In the spirit of the Renaissance man, Jerry allows us to live with him—chapter after chapter—in the realities of our complex world of difficult business decisions. He brings us into a place where we can clearly see that most decisions are never black or white—they are gray. And with gray comes the real challenges of life, particularly of organizational life.

Oh, if life were only black and white, it would be so easy! But it's not. It's full of color. Yet we too often get caught up in the black and white conflicts that make us believe we need to prove we are right. And when we feel we need to prove we are right, we fall into positional thinking, which takes us into entrenchment, which takes us into win/lose, which takes us into territoriality, which takes us into toxic workplaces. We don't experience the vitality of life or its underlying challenges and richness. We become caught in a very I-centric way of being.

As an author who has studied, researched, and written about how to create Vital We-centric workplaces, and one who has devoted almost three decades to writing my two books, *Creating We* and *The DNA of Leadership*, I know how hard it is to find words to describe the deeper challenges that pull people apart at work.

In *Managing the Gray Areas*, Jerry gives us a new lens with which to explore and understand what it takes to be a leader of the future. He frames up our workplace challenges—in a wonderful simplifying theme of black, white, and gray. For people in organizations to grow

1

together, even in the face of challenges, we need to change the conversation. It's so easy to get caught up in conflict and winning. It takes a more mature and seasoned mind to be able to hold the complexities and dialectics out in front of ourselves. We need to have the boldness to stay in a place of discovery and curiosity—examining both sides of what appear to be "fighting thoughts" so that what emerges is wisdom.

The old school of management and leadership focused on solving problems and getting to "the answer." In *Managing the Gray Areas*, we are challenged to open our minds to "both/and" thinking. This allows us to blend seemingly opposing concepts and ideas, not to decide between them; to understand relationships, not to separate them; to drive inquiry through rich questions; and to not get caught up in quick assumptions just to feel certainty. We are challenged to keep the dialogue going, to learn to hold the view open, while we leverage our collective intelligence in the pursuit of better decision making.

Through a wonderful thread of narrative and storytelling that places science alongside philosophy and history next to business, we start to see that we are at a time in the evolution of consciousness that we need to return to the wisdom of Aristotle and Socrates. At the same time, we need to go beyond these great masters of thinking to a new thinking mastery.

We need to work collectively through, inside of, and around conversations that lead us to seeing the multiple sides and perspectives of our reality. We need to break our old patterns of "telling" and get to a place where we engage with others more deeply, fully, and robustly in seeing the world from all sides.

In my book *Creating We*, I talk about "holding the space open" for vital conversations to emerge. *Managing the Gray*

Areas supports this belief and gives guidance to leaders as they work to create environments for growth and generativity of people and business. Leaders must practice engaging people in new conversations, in which we are not fighting each other to prove our reality is right. Instead we are breaking the old power-over mentality and are advocating a power-with mentality. This translates into better decision making, better people and leadership development, and work environments that harvest wisdom, not just knowledge.

Individual Needs vs. Organizational Goals, Generalists vs. Specialists, Big Picture vs. Narrow Focus, Structure vs. Flexibility, Vigilance vs. Delegation, Appearance vs. Substance, and Centralization vs. Decentralization are all constructs that we use to try to describe the underlying dynamic tensions that exist day to day as we make our choices and craft our decisions. These are not "either/or"; they are "ands." Those who master the mental and conversational flexibility to move in and out of these appearing dialectics will create a rich environment where conflict is no longer difficult—instead it is both educational and enriching. This is what we all need to learn to become infinitely more successful at business and at life.

– Judith E. Glaser
  Author of two best-selling business books: *Creating We: Change I-Thinking to WE-Thinking & Build a Healthy Thriving Organization* and *The DNA of Leadership*

I first became interested in topics such as systems thinking, emotional intelligence, and intrinsic motivation thanks to my friend Jerome Jewell. We met more than 25 years ago, when I attended one of his productivity workshops. I was intrigued by his perspectives on these matters, as well as his fundamental stance that leaders need to focus on asking better questions and setting better priorities. Over the years, we stayed in contact through e-mail. In 2006, we came to the conclusion that, as our paths had taken us in complementary areas of research, it would be worthwhile to collaborate on a new workshop. In November of 2006, that workshop came to be. Held at the National Constitution Center in Philadelphia, Pennsylvania, it was titled *The Leadership Quadrant: Four Ps for Organizational Excellence*, the four Ps being Principles, People, Productivity, and Process.

In the seminar, we facilitated dynamic leadership discussions among professionals from industries as diverse as health care, criminal intelligence, and manufacturing. In addition to the need to ask the right questions and set better priorities, we tackled topics such as leading with principles and engaging our people. We examined the challenges leaders face in trying to satisfy multiple audiences. We explored the dangers of short-term thinking at the expense of long-term organizational excellence.

As part of the seminar, the group observed *Freedom Rising*, the multimedia presentation at the Constitution Center. Through the film and the accompanying exhibits, we witnessed the struggles of an aspiring nation as it faced continuous challenges—ethical, political, and otherwise.

As expected, this generated healthy debate regarding difficult issues in today's organizations; the more we discussed, the more we realized the uniqueness of each organization, each individual, and each situation. For many of the issues, there were no clear black and white answers.

By the end of the seminar, one thing was crystal clear; as leaders, we need to make an effort to understand the potential variables involved in our decisions, striving toward "a more perfect union," knowing full well that perfection will never be achieved. From this conclusion, and from the challenging questions and valuable debates that led up to it, I knew immediately what my next book needed to be. Hence, *Managing the Gray Areas* was born.

As I progressed with writing the book, I found myself accumulating even more questions. As each question arose, I researched the topic and the many (often conflicting) viewpoints established by others. Keeping with the theme of the book, the idea was not to identify "one size fits all" solutions (management and leadership are never that easy), but to synthesize and integrate the information to serve as a guide for leaders of people, projects, and organizations. Along the way, I discovered tools and techniques that can help navigate the complexities of leadership, which I've shared in this book.

Managing the Gray Areas touches on topics such as principles, values, ethics, decision making, incentives, staffing, critical thinking, and communication. It pulls ideas from a wide variety of knowledge areas, including philosophy, science, art, medicine, business, and history. It offers educated leaders alternatives to adopting quick-fix solutions or making ill-fated assumptions. Ultimately, this is a book about leading with humanity.

Managing the Gray Areas

No matter how far you've gone on a wrong road, turn back.

- Turkish Proverb

Section I
Introduction

Chapter 1
Tough Questions for Leaders

"If a man will begin with certainties, he shall end in doubts; but if he will be content to begin with doubts, he shall end in certainties."

- Francis Bacon

Leaders face dilemmas every day. Decisions we make are translated into real-world outcomes, with each decision cascading into other actions. Sometimes, we mentally frame difficult choices and decisions in terms that simplify them—at least on the surface. We turn them into black or white just to get some clarity around them, yet in reality, they are not black or white, not either/or—they are gray.

How we address these difficult choices—as black and white, or as gray—will determine the feel of our organization. It will determine how people interact and how work gets done. It will determine the strategies of both our present and our future.

These gray areas pull us into different directions and decision paths regarding resources, time, space, functions, people, culture, and a hundred other things. How we approach these gray areas is vital to our success as leaders. Learning to live in the "gray," and dialogue about the gray with others, opens up opportunities for us as leaders to expand our thinking and to see the bigger issues from broader perspectives. In doing so, we are able to move from tactics to strategies, from either/or to unexamined possibilities, and from quick fixes to long-term solutions.

True leadership is about understanding and managing complexities instead of taking black and white or universal approaches to problems. Supporting this premise, this book explores typical challenges with which many leaders struggle, and offers a set of guidelines, principles, and tools that can help them navigate these murky waters—challenges such as:

- How can I empathize with my people's needs in the face of organizational pressures?
- When should I share the big picture with my team, and when is it prudent not to do so?
- Is it best to assemble a team of targeted specialists, or should I look for people who can do a little of everything?
- How can I implement and enforce internal processes without hurting morale or stifling creativity?
- How can I ensure adequate accountability without resorting to micromanagement?
- Given limited time and/or money, should I first focus on creating a good image for my organization, team, or product, or should I spend more time ensuring that it functions well on the back end?
- Should I centralize my organization to gain economies of scale, or should I decentralize to take advantage of local or regional expertise?

To address these questions and others, we will explore new insights from history, science, and business, as well as expert opinion from today's foremost thought leaders. We will examine concepts and tools that have been proven to aid in dealing with complexity. And we will learn to ask the right questions and to set the right priorities.

In the end, we will see that leadership is abstract—not concrete—and that applying a set of principles, guidelines, and tools, rather than relying on unilateral, all-purpose formulas, is appropriate. And while we cannot guarantee *right* answers, we can ensure that we arrive at *thoughtful* answers.

Knowledge and Wisdom

By learning to deal with the gray areas, we begin to achieve wisdom, not just knowledge. In their superb book, *Hard Facts, Dangerous Half-Truths, and Total Nonsense,* authors Jeffrey Pfeffer and Bob Sutton discuss the differences between knowledge and wisdom. "Wisdom," they say, "is about knowing what you know [i.e., knowledge] and knowing what you don't know."[1] They go on to describe how wisdom is built over time, by learning and adjusting. It also involves questioning.

Voltaire once said, "Judge a man by his questions rather than by his answers." This is especially true of anyone in a leadership position. In fact, Socrates, the father of Western philosophy, felt that we not only have a *right* to ask questions, we have a *duty* to ask questions. Socrates was considered the wisest of the wise by his followers, yet he stressed that if he was wise, it was only because he knew what he did not know. He was famous for posing challenging questions to his young disciples, teaching them to back up their claims and accept nothing as gospel. Unfortunately, he was persecuted for these very beliefs. When, in 399 B.C., Socrates was condemned to death by poison, he declared, "The unexamined life is not worth living." The Socratic line of questioning is still taught in law schools today. We'll see examples of Socratic questioning in Chapter 10.

Indeed, as Socrates and Voltaire knew, it is through asking the right questions and striving to set the right priorities that we can best achieve wisdom, not by seeking perfection and pointing fingers at those with differing opinions. We need to move away from black and white thinking and begin to acknowledge shades of gray.

A Matter of Priority...and Values

Setting the right priorities is important to all of us. Consider what noted author Ram Charan has to say in his article "Five Rules for Setting the Right Priorities" about how critical this is to an organization:

> The right priorities keep the organization's physical and emotional energy focused on the important things, in the midst of all the day-to-day stress of life at work where everything can seem urgent and important. Priorities provide clarity and focus for you—and for the people who work for you.[2]

In other words, focusing on priorities can help us navigate those ever-challenging gray areas. In his article, Charan stresses the importance of focusing on a select few priorities, communicating them frequently, ensuring you have the right people to carry out the priorities, allocating your resources to the priorities, and creating a feedback loop to make sure the message has sunk in. These actions make the priorities "real."[3]

In essence, focusing our team on priorities can help everyone see more clearly when faced with the daily challenges of life and leadership. We must also keep in mind that, in order to focus on the right priorities, we must first have a strong sense of what *values* are important to us. If we don't have a clear sense of who we are, it becomes difficult to set priorities. As we will discover later in this book, values matter.

Meeting the Challenge: Seven Gray Areas

It would be foolish to try to address all of the questions leaders might ask themselves in the course of their daily activities. Instead, we need to examine these questions through the lens of a finite set of common dilemmas.

Based on the plaguing questions I've gathered over the years, interviews with other leaders and consultants, and research on the top questions posed by today's leaders, I have identified seven gray areas with which most leaders struggle. They are as follows:

Gray Area	Fundamental Question
Individual Needs vs. Organizational Goals	How can I meet the needs of individuals *and* the needs of the organization?
Generalists vs. Specialists	How should I staff my team?
Big Picture vs. Narrow Focus	How much detail should I share with my team?
Structure vs. Flexibility	How can I maintain a sense of order without compromising productivity?
Vigilance vs. Delegation	How much can I trust the people on my team to do what they're supposed to do? Where should accountability lie?
Appearance vs. Substance	Which should I address first—appearance or substance? Where can I most afford to make sacrifices, and when?
Centralization vs. Decentralization	Which work should be done centrally and which distributed? Where should decision making lie?

For many of these gray areas, the answers may seem simple on the surface. But when we peel the onion, we will see that there are underlying complexities involved in these issues. In the coming chapters, rather than proposing simple black and white solutions and taking an either/or approach, we will examine the questions and issues that must be considered for each gray area in order to develop an integrated solution. We will see examples from multiple perspectives. And we will identify valuable principles, tools, and techniques for determining the right priorities—and promoting the right values.

Finally, as we learn these principles, tools, and techniques, we will find ourselves becoming better leaders. We will no longer adopt "one size fits all" solutions, or take rash approaches to people and problems. We will be better equipped to deal with today's complexities by setting the right priorities, which will come as a result of knowing who we are and what we stand for. And we will learn to second-guess quick-fix solutions by asking the right questions. We will look at issues more holistically and from broader perspectives. Finally, with these newfound capabilities, we will be well on our way toward managing the gray areas effectively in the real world.

Now, more than at any other time, the world needs great leaders. I invite you to join me on a journey to becoming one of them.

Key Concepts

- How we approach our choices—either as black and white, or as gray—will determine the feel of our organization. It will determine how people interact, how work gets done, and what strategies we undertake.

- By managing the gray areas, we are able to move from tactics to strategies, from either/or to unexamined possibilities, and from quick fixes to long-term solutions.

- Our job as leaders is not to have all the answers; it is to ask the right questions.

- Wisdom includes knowing what you know and what you don't know, and is built by learning and adjusting over time.

- Wise leaders focus on principles and priorities instead of "one size fits all" solutions.

- Our priorities are dictated by our values.

- Priorities can help us focus amidst the daily stresses of life and work.

? Questions to Ponder

1. Do I tend to implement sweeping policies and rules because it seems like the easiest way to manage?

2. For policies I've implemented, have I run each of them through several "use case" scenarios by various audiences to be sure they're not too rigid?

3. What is the goal of each policy? Are the policies in place the best ways to achieve those goals? Have I explored alternate solutions?

4. How much time do I spend investigating new practices or contemplating new ideas?

5. Do I encourage open discussion and seek out those with opposing perspectives?

6. Have I defined my core values and key priorities and organized my resources around them?

 **Notes**

Get even more from this book. Visit **www.rmcpublications.com/grayareas** to share your thoughts and questions on topics in this chapter and to access additional resources.

Chapter 2
Black, White, and Gray

"*The open-minded see the truth in different things; the narrow-minded see only the differences.*"

- Anonymous

There are usually multiple perceptions of the truth. Thus, the idea is not to turn gray into black or white, but to strive for appropriate shades of gray, achieving an *approximation* of the truth. We can get ever closer to perfection, but we must realize that there will inevitably be some audience or some situation that we will not be able to effectively address. The key is to address as many perspectives and situations as possible using sound principles and with the right priorities.

The problem with black and white thinking is that it usually misses the boat on taking a broad enough view. Thus, it ignores the possibility that there may be multiple perceptions of the truth.

Perhaps Austrian author Marie Ebner Von Eschenbach said it best:

Whenever two good people argue over principles, they are both right.

Indeed, if agreement is needed and a creative solution cannot be reached, one party ends up passively resisting at best and planning for conflict at worst.

In Search of Creativity

The need to demonstrate creativity when solving problems is a core principle of gray area management. For example, a popular puzzler used in leadership seminars paints an intriguing scenario:

> You are driving in a two-seater car and it begins to rain heavily. Stopped at a traffic light, you notice three people standing in the pouring rain: an elderly woman clearly in need of medical attention, a good friend that you haven't seen in years, and the love of your life. Whom would you pick up?

It's often enlightening to observe people discussing this situation. Some, based on principles of "highest need," will choose to rescue the elderly woman. Some choose their loved one. Occasionally, a creative answer will emerge that doesn't assume the solutions are mutually exclusive. Instead, it focuses on addressing all the needs, at least as well as possible. One such solution reported was to lend the car to your friend and have him or her drive the elderly woman to the hospital while you walk with the love of your life in the rain. While there is no right or wrong answer, this does give us insight into a person's thinking style. Legend has it that one organization used this question as part of their CEO hiring process to test the applicants' creative thinking skills.

Culture guru Fons Trompenaars wrote a book titled *Did the Pedestrian Die?* The title takes its name from a puzzle that he posed to thousands of workshop attendees worldwide (I've paraphrased the puzzle below):

> You were a passenger in your friend's car when he hit a pedestrian. He had been driving at least 35 miles per hour in a 20 miles per hour zone. There were no other witnesses. Your friend's lawyer states that if you testify that he was driving the speed limit, it may save him from dire consequences. [1]

Workshop attendees were asked if the friend has a definite right, some right, or no right to expect loyalty in this situation. Trompenaars found that the answer greatly depended upon the culture of the attendee, with French, Latin, and Asian cultures valuing friendship above all, and German, English, and American cultures more likely to observe the rules. Moreover, regardless of the cultural bias, if the workshop attendee found out that the pedestrian had died, it further solidified their stance.[2]

One exception was noted. A Japanese participant said that he would ask his friend to tell the truth in court, while at the same time he would plead to the judge for leniency due to his friend's honesty and misfortune. Again, this is a creative solution that attempts to reconcile seemingly opposing choices. Indeed, as Trompenaars states, the ability to integrate opposing values is essential to effective leadership.[3] In the book *Built to Last*, Jim Collins and Jerry Porras talk about "the tyranny of the OR" and "the genius of the AND."[4] When managing the gray areas, we always want to aim for *integrating* and *reconciling* opposing choices, and not assume we're faced with an either/or situation or with compromising one side or the other.

While it's important to have values—and to recognize that there may be alternate and equally compelling values—there is no doubt that creativity is a key ingredient for bridging any gaps between value systems. Later on, we'll explore tools for fostering creative thinking and for taking a more holistic view of situations.

Examples of Black and White Thinking

Black and white thinking typically ignores the middle ground and results in a rush to judgment. It also assumes one view of the truth and tends to produce "one size fits all" solutions. We see examples of this every day.

Whether it's big consulting companies touting the remedy *du jour*, government leaders imposing sweeping laws that undermine accountability and flexibility, or department managers rolling out burdensome processes, we see black and white thinking everywhere we look. Sometimes it's disguised, allegedly rooted in firm principles or beliefs. Nowhere is this more evident than in wars of ideals, which not only can happen across continents, but within a country or an organization as well.

In essence, it is a fundamental mistake to label people or ideas as good or bad. It takes critical, or "gray," thinking skills to get beyond that. Bruce Thompson, instructor of philosophy at Cuyamaca College, runs a wonderful Web site on fallacies of thinking, or what he calls "the bewildering subject of bad reasoning."[5] On the site, he lists some typical examples of black and white thinking:

Hunters and gun collectors have a perfect right to own weapons. Therefore, gun control laws of any kind are a bad idea.

My contribution to the Red Cross won't solve the problem of world hunger, so it won't do any good. I won't bother to make a contribution at all.[6]

Thompson also points out that, while reasoning using the process of elimination isn't bad in itself, black and white thinking eliminates options too quickly by assuming there is only one right answer.[7] Let's look at some further examples of black and white thinking.

Examples in Education

Dennis Littky, renowned education reformer and author of the eye-opening book *The Big Picture: Education Is Everyone's Business*, discusses black and white thinking in American education. He explains how, in 1892, a group of ten elite educational institution leaders appointed by the

National Education Association (NEA) decided that all subjects should be taught the same way to all students.[8] Despite evidence indicating that students have different learning styles and unique strengths and should be given individualized attention in small classrooms, this generic approach to education remains strong to this day.

In more than a hundred years, all we've done is make incremental "improvements" based on the same philosophy, quite possibly making our education system worse instead of better.

As another example of black and white thinking, Littky cites a report from February 2001 about a school in Minnesota that banned hugging. Overzealous school officials noticed that a few students would hug whenever they saw each other, and the officials felt the behavior was too suggestive. This brings to mind the popular legal maxim, "Hard cases make bad law"—or as Littky puts it, "You cannot make rules based on the exception."[9]

The same is true in any endeavor.

Examples in Current Events

Perhaps nothing in this world exemplifies black and white thinking more than religious intolerance—or, more precisely, clashes over ideals. Consider the situation in the Middle East, and the clashes between the Islamic and Western world. The fact is, the three major monotheistic religions, Judaism, Islam, and Christianity, share many of the same messages and even claim the same God—the God of Abraham. They do differ on the messenger, the specific traditions meant to reinforce the message, and some fundamental beliefs. As a result, many people in each of these religions remain intolerant of the others, focusing on the differences while ignoring the common core values.

Since each religion has varying degrees of orthodoxy—and many interpretations of its doctrine—this intolerance is not only directed toward other religions, but within each religion as well.

Thus, we continue to fight the same battle we've been fighting for thousands of years. For all the knowledge we've gained, we haven't gained much wisdom. Could it be that we're not asking the right questions or setting the right priorities? As it is, I don't think Jesus, Mohammed, or any other religious figure would be terribly happy with our progress.

Examples in Organizations

Black and white thinking affects people at all levels, so it should come as no surprise that such thinking is prevalent among those at the helm of organizations. For example, many leaders fall victim to the *halo effect*, a phrase coined by noted psychologist Edward Thorndike. The halo effect describes the flawed thinking that occurs when leaders make sweeping judgments about people and solutions. They tend to label others as generally good or generally bad and usually jump to conclusions about solutions to problems (e.g., this worked for company XYZ, so it must be a great solution that will work here). Often, they base their judgment on hearsay or an isolated observation. In doing this, they overlook crucial external influences and other variables, and even ignore contrary evidence.

In his compelling study *The Halo Effect... And the Eight Other Business Delusions That Deceive Managers*, author and international strategy professor Phil Rosenzweig suggests that wise managers should view problems in terms of "interlocking probabilities." As he puts it, "Their objective is not to find keys to guaranteed success, but to improve the odds through a thoughtful consideration of factors."

He suggests looking at problems holistically, using gray thinking instead of automatically assuming that certain outcomes were the result of single factors.[10] People—and problems—are more complex than that.

Forced Ranking: Black and White Thinking Exemplified

Let's look at another popular example of organizational black and white thinking—the policy of forced ranking, popularized by GE under CEO Jack Welch. Put simply, Welch instituted a policy at GE whereby employees were ranked as "A," "B," or "C" players, representing the top 20 percent, middle 70 percent, and bottom 10 percent, respectively. Each year, the "C" players were weeded out. Welch's rationale was that he needed to operate with the best people and keep the organization from growing stale. Organizations everywhere began adopting this policy, mainly because of GE's financial success. They assumed that because GE was financially successful, then everything GE did was worth emulating and that this policy must have been a direct contributor to its success.

If those organizations had conducted further research, they would have seen the flaws in this theory. In their book on evidence-based management, Pfeffer and Sutton point out three flaws in particular. First, GE's policy ignores the concept that people's performance is often dependent on other people and on external factors out of their control. (We will discuss this concept further in Chapter 7.) Second, as a survey conducted by the Novations Group of more than 200 human resource professionals showed, forced ranking (a practice employed by more than half of the companies surveyed) results in lower productivity, injustice, skepticism, less employee engagement, reduced collaboration, lower morale, and mistrust in leadership.

Finally, Pfeffer and Sutton have this to say about forced ranking:

> If an organization selects and trains people right, and places them in an effective system, there is no reason why 10 percent or 20 percent would automatically become incompetent every year.[11]

Automatically is the operative word. Of course, even Pfeffer and Sutton acknowledge that it is indeed valid—and necessary—to root out those who consistently display negative or disruptive behavior, do not embrace organizational initiatives, or perform poorly. But it is shortsighted to do this in an automatic or formulaic fashion, or to mandate a quota. Jack Welch did many things worth emulating. Forced ranking is not one of them.

Why Do People Think in Black and White?

In his article "Black and White Thinking Doesn't Work in a Gray World," pastor and syndicated columnist Byron Williams summed up nicely why people tend to think in terms of black and white:

> To see the world in black and white is to live within the contours of extremism. This outlook neatly divides the world into right versus wrong, good versus evil, and yes versus no. This thinking is dependent upon such words as always and never. Especially in times of crisis, the black and white world view is looked upon as strength and courage to the casual observer. [12]

Of course, as Williams points out, classic American films further reinforce this view, with clear lines drawn between good and evil, and heroes and villains.[13] Even in films, however, characters are said to have more depth if "good" characters have some negative traits, and vice versa.

In other words, if they're not black and white, they appear more *realistic*.

Williams goes on to show how children learn through this cognitive style and are often confused when a parent changes a rule ever so slightly. As he points out, in developmental psychology this is referred to as primitive thinking. As adults, we often resort to this mode of thinking when confused or faced with a crisis.[14] Consider what Carmine Coyote, who runs a Weblog called Slow Leadership, has to say:

> When people feel stressed or harassed, especially if they feel they have no time beyond the minimum, something has to go. That something is usually complexity or subtlety. Faced with making decisions quickly, no matter how uncertain or complicated, people fall back on black or white thinking...Many leaders today are addicted to it.[15]

Coyote calls black and white thinking "the mental equivalent of sucking your thumb."[16] When faced with a "fight or flight" situation, this way of thinking may be an understandable defense mechanism, but for most complex leadership decisions, black and white thinking is not the optimal response. On the contrary, it is in times of crisis that we most need to think in shades of gray.

Taking the Middle Ground

Ironically, while we often use black and white thinking to protect us from danger, the "all or nothing" view that it takes can cause us more psychological harm than good. By looking at a situation as dire or unrecoverable, or a person as evil or no good, we spawn a vicious cycle of emotions. Not only can this contribute to a depressed state, but we depress others as well. Indeed, when we look at situations and people more closely, there are always elements of good and bad and many variables to be considered. We want to avoid words such as *always, never, impossible, terrible, failure, ruined,* and *furious.*[17]

The bottom line is that we must acknowledge that there may be other realities than what meets the eye. The Depression Learning Path Web site, an online resource from the United Kingdom, offers this set of questions to stimulate gray area thinking:

Can I be basically an intelligent person and still do something stupid?

Can I love my children and still get angry with them sometimes?

Can my partner love me but sometimes be insensitive?

Can one part of my life be difficult and other parts be easier and more enjoyable?

Can a part of my life be difficult now but in the future get easier?

Can some parts of an experience (such as a social engagement or vacation) be awful and other parts of it be OK?[18]

If we apply this same line of thinking to our business problems, we'll be less apt to make rash decisions and sweeping judgments. We'll look at situations more positively, creating a brighter work environment as well.

The Challenge of Gray Area Management

Ralph Waldo Emerson once said, "A foolish consistency is the hobgoblin of little minds." By now, we can begin to see the truth in this. But how do we take the time to consider all the variables when making tough decisions at the speed of light? How do we navigate the complexities?

I recently attended a lecture on self-awareness and influence by Dr. Charles Dwyer, Academic Director of the

Aresty Institute's Leading and Managing People program in the Wharton School. I was so impressed with his
insights on values and influencing people that I bought his
book, *The Shifting Sources of Power and Influence*. As expected,
the book was an eye-opener and a jewel for anyone in leadership. In the book, Dwyer identifies three major realities
we all face as leaders:

Reality	Description
Dissonant Value Systems	People have conflicting value systems, a fact made even more visible by the advent of the Internet and global access to media.
Diffused Power	As organizations grow ever larger, and as concepts such as decentralization and special interest groups spread, power is distributed in a matrix fashion.
Limited Resources	We all face a limited set of resources, made even more challenging by our lack of willingness to accept tradeoffs or a good mechanism to guide operational priorities.

19

Indeed, when faced with conflicting value systems,
distributed power, and limited resources, a leader's job
becomes abstract and quite complex. Concrete black and
white thinking simply won't cut it. We have entered the
realm of the gray, for which there is no single formula.

There *are*, however, principles and tools that can help
us set the right priorities, ask the right questions, and
become better leaders. And that is what we will continue
to explore in the remainder of this book.

Key Concepts

- Wise leaders understand that there may be multiple views of the truth.

- Creative thinking can help bridge the gaps between competing values.

- When faced with opposing choices, it is preferable to integrate or reconcile them rather than deciding between one or the other.

- While process of elimination is a sound concept, black and white thinkers eliminate options too quickly.

- Evidence shows that students have different strengths and learning styles, and need individualized attention. Employees are no different.

- Rules should not be based on the exception.

- A key conflict management strategy is to look for common ground.

- Situations are best considered in context, examining all the variables instead of resorting to "all or nothing" thinking, or using words such as *always*, *never*, or *ruined*.

- The halo effect occurs when we label others as good or bad and jump to conclusions about solutions to problems.

- Forced ranking of people or judging them based on a quota or formula is often inaccurate and can lead to lower morale and less employee engagement.

- When faced with conflicting value systems, distributed power, and limited resources, a leader's job becomes more complex. This requires principles, tools, priorities, and asking the right questions—not quick-fix solutions.

? Questions to Ponder

1. In what ways can I become more aware of people's individual strengths and learning styles? What policies do I have that ignore this aspect of human nature?

2. Do I make rules based on the exception? How can I avoid doing so in the future?

3. How can I find common ground among those with whom I am in conflict? What are some creative solutions that will meet the most important needs of all parties?

4. Do I look at problems holistically, considering a complex combination of external influences, situations, and events—or do I point fingers and make generalizations about the people that I believe have caused the problem?

5. Do I view individuals on my team as "good people" or "bad people," or do I try to understand their underlying complexities and motivating factors?

6. Do I tend to use words like *always, never, failure,* and other "all or nothing" words? Are these words truly accurate? If not, what are some alternative ways of looking at situations?

 Notes

Get even more from this book. Visit **www.rmcpublications.com/grayareas** to share your thoughts and questions on topics in this chapter and to access additional resources.

Section II
Seven Gray Areas

Chapter 3
Individual Needs vs. Organizational Goals

*"Our country is not the only thing to which we owe our
allegiance. It is also owed to justice and to humanity."*
- James Bryce

Fundamental Question:
How can I meet the needs of individuals *and* the needs of the organization?

One of the core challenges of leadership is to address the needs of multiple audiences while trying to help an organization achieve its goals. To aid us in meeting this challenge, we must first realize that an organization is a collection of individuals brought together by its leaders, each with their own needs and biases, to achieve a common set of objectives (or so one would hope). These individuals—including our direct staff and other managers—have their own personal needs, which may or may not be aligned with the goals of the organization. Our job as leaders is to understand those needs and, as Charles Dwyer suggests, to influence those individuals to invest in *our* needs in order to meet *theirs*.[1] It's a tricky business.

In 1943, renowned psychologist Abraham Maslow defined a hierarchy of needs that we all seek to satisfy, going from the most basic to the most fulfilling. In order, they are: physiological, safety/security, social (love/belonging), esteem, and self-actualization. From a business perspective, psychologist Frederick Herzberg later categorized the first three—in the form of job-related issues such as salary, relationships with others, job security, status, and personal life—as "hygiene factors" that people assume will exist. They do not serve as motivators in themselves, but a lack of any of them becomes a demotivator. The last two, esteem (recognition/respect) and self-actualization (leveraging one's unique talents) are indeed motivators, with self-actualization being the ultimate satisfier.

In their landmark book *First, Break All the Rules*, Marcus Buckingham and Curt Coffman recognize this need for self-actualization, stating that a manager's *primary role* is to leverage individuals' strengths to meet organizational goals.[2] Moreover, it is absolutely futile to try to get someone to go against their very nature in our attempts to make them fit some ideal model. There is great truth in the oft-quoted line from author Robert Heinlein, "Never try to teach a pig to sing; it wastes your time and annoys the pig."

In line with this approach, Buckingham and Coffman suggest that managers have four obligations:

1. Selecting people based on their natural strengths (as opposed to merely knowledge or skills)
2. Focusing on expectations and outcomes (as opposed to rules or steps)
3. Motivating people with specific praise and recognition
4. Developing people by helping them grow in their existing areas of strength[3]

Indeed, through this emphasis on strengths, we can meet the needs of both the individuals on our team *and* the organization as a whole.

The concept of aligning teams around people's natural talents is not an entirely new one, although Buckingham and Coffman have taken it to a new level. Legendary management guru Peter Drucker long ago declared, "The task of leadership is to create an alignment of strengths, making our weaknesses irrelevant." Drucker knew that by managing around people's limitations, we'd face fewer barriers, avoid unnecessary frustration, and gain productivity. As Albert Einstein said, "Once we accept our limits, we go beyond them."

Of course, aligning people with their strengths is often easier said than done. Perhaps you have a staff member who no longer enjoys performing a role they happen to be good at. Or maybe you have a team member who is passable in their current role, but who lacks some key strength required to take the role to the next level. Although you have a duty to be a decent human being and take care of your people, you're also there to serve the organization and its customers. How do you walk that fine line?

There's no black and white answer, but there *are* some guidelines that can help us.

To Do No Harm

Primum non nocere is a Latin phrase that means, "First, do no harm." It is believed that Hippocrates, the father of medicine, originated the phrase in the fourth century B.C., in his book *Of the Epidemics* (particularly Book I). The premise is that, before taking action, we must consider the harm that our intervention may cause versus the benefit it will bring. Not only that, but we must consider the impact to all parties. In the cases mentioned previously—the staff member who wants to switch jobs and the team member who is merely passable—we need to examine the situations considering the needs of the individual, the organization, and the customer, as well as the harm that may be caused to each by our choice of action.

A brief ethics lesson could serve us well here. In his book *Ethics for Everyone*, author Arthur Dobrin describes three schools of thought regarding ethics. *Virtue ethics*, popularized by Aristotle, focuses on the personal character traits to which we strive to adhere. *Consequentialist ethics*, which British philosopher John Stewart Mill endorsed in the form of utilitarianism, takes a more pragmatic approach and primarily looks at results. Lastly, *principled ethics*, popularized by Immanuel Kant, bases decisions on what are believed to be universal, unbendable principles.[4]

As Dobrin points out, each approach—virtue ethics, consequentialist ethics, and principled ethics—has limitations, so it's best to consider all three holistically when making decisions.[5]

Holistic Ethics

Let's take the case of the staff member who wants to switch from a job the individual excels at to a role he or she is not quite qualified for. Using virtue ethics, we might try to determine what we need to do in order to satisfy our most desired character traits, such as integrity, courage, justice, or some other quality we hold dear. Using consequentialist ethics, we might examine the potential results of several alternate solutions, such as giving the person the role, denying the person the role, or helping to find them a new job. Using principled ethics, we might try to uphold the principle of "Do no harm," provided we can determine, for each scenario, the level of potential harm caused to the individual versus the organization. Any one of these ethics approaches might miss the boat, yet together, they are powerful. We can call this combined approach *holistic ethics*.

Holistic Ethics	
Virtue Ethics	What do I stand for? What values drive me?
Consequentialist Ethics	What would be the outcome, for the many and the few?
Principled Ethics	What is "right"? What am I obligated to do?

Using holistic ethics, we examine all sides of the issue. Would switching the individual to the desired new role harm the organization? If so, what would be the impact of the damage, and for how long? Does the person have natural talents that would fit the new position once the appropriate skills and knowledge are achieved? If not, are there ways to make up for the person's weaknesses by providing a tool or pairing them with someone who has offsetting strengths? Does the individual have a positive "can do" attitude, to the point where it may be worth making some minor sacrifices in order to retain them?

The same process applies to our other scenario, in which we have a team member who is just passable in their current role. We're not talking about a complete slacker—that would be too easy. More precisely, let's assume the person is what Jack Welch might consider a "B" player, at least for the role we have them in. That's more typical of a gray area challenge most leaders face.

It's clear that we have an obligation to assemble the best team to meet the organization's objectives. Not many leaders would argue that fact. However, is it acceptable to have players on our team that are merely *adequate* if they've "done no harm"? Keep in mind that this individual might have a family to support, bills to pay, and a sick relative they're taking care of. Does this change the situation any?

The answer will depend on our personal values, the culture we live in, the principles that guide us, the results we are trying to achieve, and a number of other variables.

Dobrin offers an eight-step approach that incorporates all three types of ethics and can help us navigate these murky waters (I've summarized them for simplicity):

1. Understand all the facts.
2. Make reasonable assumptions about the information that's missing.
3. Interpret the facts based on the values that are important to you.
4. Understand the problem through the eyes of all parties involved.
5. Plot out the possible consequences of each course of action, weighing the potential harm versus the potential good.
6. Examine your feelings. You may find something that logic will overlook.
7. Think about how you will feel with each decision.
8. Think about how you will justify this decision to others.[6]

As for our scenario, we can assume that maintaining a team of only the best people (i.e., "A" players) will be an exercise in futility at best and cause negative repercussions at worst. As mentioned earlier, arbitrarily weeding out players leads to less engagement and low morale. In this case, it's not quite arbitrary, since the person may lack certain skills we need. Even so, before we consider replacing our people, we have a duty as leaders to ensure we're getting the best out of our people. It's the difference between being an impatient leader versus an enlightened one. To be an enlightened leader, we must learn to lead with justice and humanity.

Leading with Justice and Humanity

Leading with justice and humanity is not the same as being a pushover. On the contrary, we have an obligation to fix performance problems, but we must do so fairly. In his book *Fixing Performance Problems*, executive coach Bud Bilanich suggests that there are eleven reasons why employees don't do what they're supposed to do, and most of the reasons are not the fault of the employee (the list was influenced by the writings of training and education guru Robert Mager). Bilanich, also known as "The Common Sense Guy" (visit his popular Web site at www.commonsenseguy.com), proposes that we rule out all eleven reasons. They are:

1. People don't know *what* they're supposed to do.
2. People don't know *why* they should do what they are supposed to do.
3. People don't know *how* to do what they're supposed to do.
4. People think the prescribed methods will not (or do not) work, or they believe that their way is better.
5. People think other things are more important.
6. People think they are performing in an acceptable manner.
7. Nonperformance is rewarded.
8. Good performance feels like punishment.
9. There are no positive consequences for good performance.
10. There are no negative consequences for poor performance.
11. There are obstacles to performing that the individual cannot control.[7]

Note that points 4, 5, and 6 refer to instances in which people may think their way is better, other things are more important, or they are performing acceptably. It may be beneficial to confirm that they are not, in fact, correct. Sometimes, being closer to the action, our employees have a better sense of what is needed than we do. When in doubt, ask them to make a case, stating why their opinion is correct. One of the greatest managers I ever worked for made a habit of doing that, and on more than one occasion, he deferred to my judgment, thanking me for speaking up.

Also, note that negative consequences aren't addressed until point 10. That's because bad systems and poor communication are more frequently at fault than bad people. Indeed, before assuming poor performance is the fault of the employee, we owe it to the employee—and to ourselves as leaders—to rule out the other reasons. I can think of no better way to lead with justice and humanity, thus serving the needs of the individual and the organization.

Speaking of negative consequences, Bilanich suggests that a simple reminder may be adequate. He often likes to tell the story of a whispered speech that Sam Jones uttered to Bill Russell after Russell missed a crucial foul shot during the final moments of the 1968 NBA Eastern Division basketball playoffs (the Boston Celtics were facing the Philadelphia 76ers). After the speech, Russell made the next foul shot to win the game. The big news story that followed was, "What were the magic words that Sam Jones uttered to Bill Russell?" Eventually, it came out. The magic words were:

Flex your knees, Bill.

Often, that's all it takes.

Avoiding Biases

We began this chapter with the concept of focusing on people's strengths and thus managing around their weaknesses. We then examined how to apply holistic ethics—that is, ethics that consider personal character, results, and good principles. We also discussed guidelines for addressing performance problems effectively and fairly. Collectively, these actions can help us balance the needs of our people with the needs of the organization. But there are still a few more guidelines that can help us in this area.

For example, we need to beware of biases. As Pfeffer and Sutton note in their book on evidence-based management, studies of the National Basketball Association have shown that players picked earlier in drafts and paid more money were less likely to be traded and had longer careers, regardless of their actual performance.[8] They were simply perceived as better because they were branded and labeled as such. They were expected to be better. This is a perfect example of the halo effect that we discussed in Chapter 2.

The same bias often happens in business. A manager will sometimes stand by an employee simply because the person has an advanced degree, they came from a reputable company, they were recommended by someone else, or any number of reasons. Likewise, the reverse may be true. We can develop negative biases toward someone for the opposite reasons. If we are to be fair and just leaders, we must be careful that these biases do not permeate our thinking process. We must lead with integrity.

Maintaining Integrity

One of the challenges leaders often face—and this is especially true of middle managers—is to do the right thing amid pressure to do otherwise. This pressure can come from all sides, and above and below. Whether we're defending our people, defending the right plan, or defending the need for systemic changes, we must strive to lead with reliability, fairness, and honesty. As management guru Tom Peters puts it, "There is no such thing as a minor lack of integrity." In his presentations, Peters has been known to quote famed fighter pilot and military strategist Colonel John Boyd, who once said:

> If your boss demands loyalty, give him integrity. But if he demands integrity, give him loyalty.

Indeed, integrity is a crucial element of meeting individual and organizational needs. Frequently, this requires making difficult decisions and standing up to some tough opposition.

Leadership expert John C. Maxwell wrote a compelling book titled *The 360 Degree Leader* about managing from anywhere in the organization. In the book, he talks about the challenges of leading from the middle of an organization, including dealing with limited authority, wearing many hats, following an ineffective leader, and other common frustrations. He discusses the principles required for leading up, leading across, and leading down. The number one principle he lists for leading up is "Lead yourself exceptionally well." This includes managing your emotions, your time, your priorities, your energy, your thinking, your words, and your personal life. Other suggestions Maxwell has for leading up are:

- Tell leaders what they need to hear, not what they want to hear.
- Plan ahead, and don't waste your leader's time.
- Always offer a solution when presenting a problem.
- Understand your leader's personality, preferences, dreams, likes, and dislikes. Relationships count.
- Master the art of knowing when to push and when to back off.[9]

Nobody said integrity was easy.

Satisfying the Customer

At this point, some may wonder where the customer fits in with all of this. After all, doesn't an organization exist to serve its customers? Hal Rosenbluth, former chairman and CEO of Rosenbluth International and coauthor of *The Customer Comes Second*, suggests that it's not quite that simple. Rosenbluth grew his business from a $20 million travel company to a $6 billion global organization before selling it to American Express in 2003. He did it by focusing on his people first and his customers second. As Rosenbluth says:

> *Companies are only fooling themselves when they believe that "The Customer Comes First." People do not inherently put the customer first, and they certainly don't do it because their employer expects it.*[10]

He goes on to clarify that this is different from choosing your people over your customers. On the contrary, he suggests that by focusing on our people's needs, we are thus taking the most effective route to satisfying our customers and boosting profits.[11]

There have been numerous studies demonstrating the value of this approach, perhaps best depicted by what experts call a *Virtuous Circle*. For example, by training and empowering our employees, we increase their satisfaction and confidence, which in turn leads to superior service, higher customer retention, and, ultimately, higher sales and profits. This creates more funding for employee development initiatives.

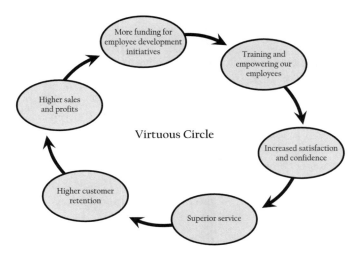

The opposite has also been demonstrated in what is called a *Vicious Circle*. Instead of focusing on developing employees and new products, management focuses on cutting costs or appeasing shareholders and executives. This results in less money for employee wages, training, and product improvements, which in turn leads to stagnant products, lower morale, more mistakes, and, ultimately, lower profits. Then, with lower profits, the cycle begins all over again.

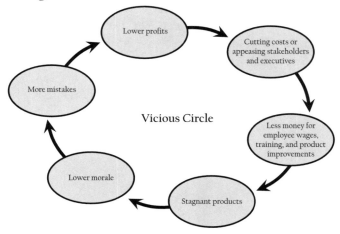

Unfortunately, many organizations, lacking courage and/or integrity, choose the latter path.

As for the customer, even there we have a dilemma between satisfying individuals and satisfying the organization (in this case, the customer's organization). For example, let's examine the question "Who is the customer?" Is it the payer, the end user, or the champion for your product or service? They may be different people with different agendas. As Keith Merron, change guru and author of *Consulting Mastery*, points out, we must look at an organization holistically.[12] Thus, the "customer" is any part of the organization that our work may impact, positively or negatively. In fact, the payer, the end user, or the champion may have desires that are in direct conflict with the organization's needs.

The dilemma becomes, "Do we do what the customer wants or what the customer needs?" Merron advises that we must sometimes walk the delicate line of showing the customer where he or she may be unwittingly participating in the very dynamics he or she wants changed.[13] We owe it to the customer *and* their organization to raise the tough issues.

One tool that can help is Quality Function Deployment (QFD), a group decision-making technique designed in the early 1960s by Drs. Yoji Akao and Shigero Mizuno. QFD was later designated as a key component of the Six Sigma quality model. The purpose of QFD is to align development or engineering characteristics with prioritized customer needs. The approach, which is best done in group settings but can also work via electronic surveys, is as follows:

1. Identify key stakeholders.
2. Prioritize the stakeholders (some stakeholders may be impacted by the outcome more than others).
3. Develop an understanding of the stakeholders' spoken and unspoken needs.

4. Identify "Expected Quality or Requirements" (items that the customer would expect to exist) vs. "Unexpected Quality or Requirements" (items that can "wow" the customer). In QFD, both are valued.

5. Document, prioritize, and gain agreement on the requirements, taking stakeholder priority into account.

6. Identify actions and design features that map to the requirements.

7. Prioritize the actions and design features based on how closely they align with the requirements.

8. Identify the top "Critical to Quality" (CTQ) actions and design features.

9. Develop a plan for implementation, always maintaining alignment with the stakeholder needs, and CTQ items.

While this approach can be valuable, organizational culture plays a part in its success. For organizations not accustomed to effective group facilitation, the process could get bogged down or be misapplied. In such cases, it may be best to bring in an experienced facilitator.

Fostering a Cohesive Organization

Thus far, we have explored how to meet the needs of the individuals on our team and the needs of our direct customers. We must also, however, consider the needs of other stakeholders—our peers and those higher in our organization. This can be an even greater challenge. More and more, organizational goals take a back seat to cross-departmental squabbles, power struggles, and individual agendas.

Antoine de Saint-Exupéry, the French writer, famous for his book *The Little Prince*, once said, "Life has taught us that love does not consist in gazing at each other, but in looking outward together in the same direction." The same sentiment can be applied to leading people. We must influence others to look outward together in the same direction. More recently, leadership author Patrick Lencioni wrote an excellent book, *Silos, Politics, and Turf Wars*, which deals with this very issue.

To get people to work more effectively together, Lencioni suggests that we find one thematic goal—a rallying cry that will unite everyone in the organization toward a common purpose. Not any old goal will do. The usual objectives of cutting costs, improving productivity, increasing quality, and the like, are what Lencioni calls *standard operating objectives*. These objectives are fine in themselves but would not suffice as a rallying cry that could get anyone excited. Instead, the thematic goal should represent a burning need that must be addressed as quickly as possible, for instance to reestablish credibility in the market within a given timeframe or to reposition the company around a certain theme. Lencioni suggests that we support the thematic goal with four to six defining objectives to be reached (each acting as a building block toward achieving the thematic goal) and several specific measures as indicators of success. Such metrics can simply be dates by which to achieve the objectives, or they can be quantifiable targets. Lencioni wisely cautions against setting arbitrary numerical targets for that which cannot be quantified.[14]

In our attempts to find a thematic goal, let's not forget that just because we announce a goal, no matter how compelling it may be, people will not automatically embrace it. If we can involve people in crafting the goal, all the better. At the least, we must involve people in creating the defining objectives. As leadership development expert Judith E. Glaser notes in her book *The DNA of Leadership*, cocreation is the ultimate way to achieve engagement.[15] It is also the best way to reconcile individual and organizational needs.

For those people who may not have been involved in cocreating the goal, we need to *influence* them to strive toward meeting that goal, which is a more difficult undertaking. We must then gain an understanding of their needs and fears—and address those needs and fears. If we do that while simultaneously making them feel the need for our stated goal, we'll be well on our way toward fostering a cohesive organization.

Key Concepts

- As leaders, we must influence people to satisfy *our* needs in order to meet *theirs*. To do this, we need to understand their needs and values.

- By focusing on our people's individual strengths and managing around their weaknesses, we can meet the needs of the individuals *and* the organization.

- Arthur Dobrin's eight-step decision-making process enables us to apply holistic ethics and to ensure that we are considering our personal values, potential implications of our actions, and proven accepted principles. In meeting the needs of the organization and our people, we have a duty to fix performance problems quickly and fairly.

- Bud Bilanich's eleven-step "Fixing Performance Problems" checklist can be used to ensure that we have ruled out communication problems and other misunderstandings before considering other causes of performance problems.

- If a team member disagrees with your instructions, they may be right. They should be given an opportunity to make their case.

- If a problem turns out to be the fault of the team member, sometimes a gentle reminder is all that's needed.

- Positive or negative biases based on assumptions, hearsay, or brief observation are to be avoided.

- Managing *oneself* well, including emotions, priorities, and words, is the first step to making and communicating decisions with integrity.

- By treating our people well, we are ultimately creating customer loyalty, customer retention, and profits (the Virtuous Circle). This results in more money to spend on employee development. The Vicious Circle—cutting costs or appeasing executives and shareholders—has the opposite effect.

- We must look at customers holistically, satisfying their organizational needs rather than blindly delivering what an individual requests.

- The Quality Function Deployment (QFD) model described in this chapter promotes a systems approach to satisfying customer needs. This model requires effective group facilitation techniques.

- Creating a single goal—a rallying cry—supported by objectives and measures, can serve to align all individuals in an organization around a common cause.

- Having people cocreate goals and objectives is the best way of ensuring engagement, and thus integrating individual and organizational needs.

❓ Questions to Ponder

1. Do I announce goals and missions and assume my team will follow them, or do I try to understand what they need to satisfy their values, desires, and concerns? Do I paint a picture whereby the organizational goals will satisfy my team members' values in some way?

2. Do I spend time trying to fix people's weaknesses instead of finding ways to leverage their strengths? How can I better make use of their strengths and manage around their weaknesses?

3. Do I rule out communication and other issues before I judge people?

4. Are there people about whom I've made assumptions—either positive or negative—because of certain expectations, hearsay, or an isolated observation?

5. How can I foster an environment where my team members feel engaged in cocreation? How can I absorb them in "looking outward together in the same direction"?

Notes

Get even more from this book. Visit **www.rmcpublications.com/grayareas** to share your thoughts and questions on topics in this chapter and to access additional resources.

Chapter 4

Generalists vs. Specialists

"I suppose it is tempting, if the only tool you have is a hammer, to treat everything as if it were a nail."
                                             - Abraham Maslow

Fundamental Question:
How should I staff my team?

Organizations often struggle with whether to hire and train people as generalists or to assemble a team of targeted specialists. Furthermore, those that go the specialist route struggle with whether the specialty should be based on skill (i.e., excellence in analysis, design, or some other talent) or knowledge (i.e., subject matter expertise).

Studies show that organizations are mixed in their approach to this issue. Some organizations choose to staff their team with mostly generalists, either to allow for greater flexibility or because they feel they can't afford the luxury of having a team of specialists. They expect these generalists to be able to handle everything from business analysis to leadership, facilitation, and more. Other organizations believe that specialists are required in order to get the "very best" out of each role on their team.

There's no easy answer. Much depends on the situation, the people involved, their work preferences, the nature of the initiative, and other factors. However, there *are* guidelines we can use to ensure that we assemble the right team for our needs. And that is what we'll discuss next. Let's begin by exploring the strengths and weaknesses of generalists and specialists.

Generalists: Strengths and Weaknesses

Because their knowledge is broad, generalists carry many advantages over those whose focus is limited to a single specialty. Generalists tend to understand the big picture by virtue of their ability to integrate knowledge from a wide variety of sources. In his book *The Customer Comes Second,* Hal Rosenbluth refers to this as *cross-pollination.*[1] In essence, the more someone is exposed to multiple areas, the greater his or her ability to synthesize the information and, thus, provide a valuable service.

Organizational leadership expert Fred Nickols, a prolific writer and founder of Distance Consulting, states that because of exposure to multiple areas, generalists are often able to offer creative solutions and are best equipped to perform initial diagnoses of problems.[2] This is especially true of problems that have not yet been isolated to one specific area. All of this, of course, assumes they have a penchant toward systems thinking (i.e., the ability to understand crucial interrelationships when solving problems) and they have the raw ingredients to be successful. In essence, their broad exposure increases the likelihood that they'll make the right connections.

With their wide-ranging experience, it comes as no surprise that generalists, especially those who excel at communication and negotiation, are the employees most often targeted for leadership. Accordingly, it is wise to select and nurture generalists who possess these talents.

One might conclude from all of this that it is best to staff your team with all generalists, but that's not necessarily so. Generalists can get stuck when more depth of knowledge is needed in certain areas. Even if a generalist has depth of knowledge in a particular area, their overall performance can suffer if they get dragged too deeply into any one activity at the expense of other duties. Generalists cannot afford to dive in too deep by virtue of their broad responsibilities.

The paradox is, by not diving in deep, generalists can sometimes oversimplify theories and miss crucial particulars. This is where the specialist comes in. While the generalist focuses on the big picture, the specialist's realm is the details.

Specialists: Strengths and Weaknesses

As noted by Fred Nickols, specialists tend to be better at implementing a solution that has already been identified as being in their area of specialty. This is not to say that specialists cannot think broadly, but, as Nickols points out, it is often best to have generalists examine the big picture until one or more specialty areas can be targeted.[3]

The benefit that specialists provide is that they have gained deep expertise through repetition and concentration. For example, a cardiac surgeon, after performing the same types of operations over and over, knows what to expect. An entertainment lawyer understands the finer points of the entertainment industry, whereas another type of lawyer may not. A consultant who specializes in business continuity, a field that deals with ensuring adequate business operations in the event of a major disaster, would likely think of potential issues that a general consultant might overlook.

Through repetition and concentration, specialists develop over time, becoming true experts in their fields of specialty. Because of this, some organizations attempt to build a team of specialists with complementary skills, hoping to end up with the equivalent of a supercharged assembly line. This may be fine for areas that require prescriptive processes and do not involve interaction, but for those that demand cooperation across multiple domains, it falls short. What's missing is the glue.

Here's the issue. Because of the focused nature of their work, specialists don't always communicate well with others, often preferring (or needing) to work heads-down in their areas of specialty. In extreme cases, their very expertise sometimes causes them to lose patience when explaining problems to those less knowledgeable. In addition, they may ignore—or even discredit—areas outside of their domain. These reactions can lead to shortsighted solutions that are framed based on a single area of expertise. Furthermore, if multiple specialists working on the same problem don't communicate, they can end up duplicating efforts or conflicting with one another.

It is clear that better integration is needed—both among specialists and between generalists and specialists.

Integration: The Missing Link

There are three significant areas in which we can improve integration: building better rapport, managing handoffs, and addressing potential gaps.

Rapport is a vital, and often overlooked, element of successful outcomes. A recent article in *CIO Magazine* by M. Eric Johnson tells of a dental product company, Align Technology, which learned some hard lessons regarding the need for rapport.[4] Align has dental technicians and orthodontists in Costa Rica who provide treatment plans for doctors in the United States, utilizing plastic dental alignment devices made in Mexico.

As the company grew, doctors in the U.S. began getting randomly assigned technicians with each call to Costa Rica, and they had to restate their preferences each time. Consequently, the number of errors increased. Align added quality checks, but that only slowed things down and added conflicts rooted in bureaucracy. It wasn't until frustrated doctors started migrating to other suppliers that Align realized they were missing a key ingredient— rapport. They began matching technicians with specific doctors, which led to smoother collaboration and greater trust. The doctors returned to Align once again.[5]

The ability to know people's preferences is critical to effective collaboration. For example, if a family practitioner understands that a specialist with whom he or she is working tends to be conservative, this knowledge becomes part of the practitioner's decision criteria. If the two individuals don't know each other well, this key input is lost. Rapport matters. We should strive to establish this rapport within our teams, across teams, and with our customers.

The second area for improving integration is what we might call handoff management. While there is great benefit to minimizing handoffs in any process (as Michael Hammer and James Champy illustrated in *Reengineering the Corporation*[6]), there will always be handoffs between generalists and specialists. The broader the problem, the more handoffs there will likely be. To minimize the damage, some suggest requiring telephone conversations the first time two people discuss a problem.[7] Organizations have developed handoff policies, with an accompanying checklist to validate that both parties are on the same page. In addition, a generalist can serve as a coordinator, managing handoffs across a multitude of specialists. Having a central coordinator also helps to avoid a fragmented customer experience. All of these ideas can help to manage handoffs more effectively, as this is where much information gets lost.

Even with rapport and handoff management, there will still be gaps left between the generalists' broad knowledge and the specialists' focused expertise. This takes us to our third area for improving integration—identifying the gaps left by narrow focus and faulty assumptions. Just as a publisher has fact-checkers to confirm the integrity of an author's material prior to publication, we need ways to address the integrity of the data that goes into decision making. Above all, we need to be sure that the data is inclusive and based on sound reasoning.

British psychologist Gordon Rugg has devised a process called the *Verifier Approach*, specifically meant to address such gaps in thinking. Using the Verifier Approach, Rugg was able to crack a 400-year-old code, the Voynich manuscript, that specialists—including linguists, cryptographers, historians, and other scholars—hadn't been able to decipher since its discovery in 1912. Even the U.S. Army code-breakers during World War II couldn't crack it.[8]

Rugg began by mapping all the areas that were currently being researched and looking for gaps in thinking. He identified one area that wasn't even conceived of—the idea that the document might be a hoax. Proceeding down that avenue, he began researching ancient encoding devices and methods and was able to account for many of the anomalies inherent in the document. His hoax theory was published and is now the generally accepted view on the Voynich manuscript. Most importantly, his approach is gaining support as a superior method for verifying gaps in problem solving. He's now being called upon to apply his research to Alzheimer's disease, which makes an ideal candidate for the Verifier Approach, with potential causes ranging from environmental toxins, smoking, drinking, lack of exercise, blows to the head, certain proteins, and any number of other factors.[9]

Rugg's Verifier Approach can serve as a useful tool for generalists, who can use it to validate gaps left by specialists. The Verifier Approach has seven steps, as follows:

1. Amass knowledge of a discipline through interviews and reading.
2. Use mental mapping to determine whether critical expertise has yet to be applied in the field.
3. Look for bias and mistakenly held assumptions in the research.
4. Analyze jargon to uncover differing definitions of key terms.
5. Check for classic mistakes using human-error tools.
6. Follow the errors as they ripple through underlying assumptions.
7. Suggest new avenues for research that emerge from steps 1 through 6.[10]

When dealing with item 3 (looking for bias and false assumptions) and item 5 (checking for other classic mistakes), there are a number of resources at our disposal. Philosophy professor Bruce Thompson maintains an excellent list of human errors and fallacies of thinking on his Web site at Cuyamaca College, arranged in a useful grid (see http://www.cuyamaca.edu/brucethompson/Fallacies/fallacies_grid.asp). This offers a wealth of examples that can aid in using Rugg's model. There's also an excellent list of cognitive biases on Wikipedia at http://en.wikipedia.org/wiki/List_of_cognitive_biases.

Indeed, by appointing someone to address gaps in thinking, and creating an environment that fosters rapport and manages handoffs, we can go a long way toward leveraging generalists and specialists more effectively. We can supercharge these efforts by including all relevant parties in our analysis and planning processes as well.

Staffing Your Team

From what we've learned so far, it seems that the ideal staffing solution is to hire generalists for areas that require broad problem solving and customer interaction, and specialists for areas that require depth of knowledge. Then we ensure that they work effectively together and *voila!* Instant teamwork! Well, it's not quite that simple. There are a number of other factors to consider.

First, whether we will be more successful with mostly generalists, mostly specialists, or some other arrangement greatly depends upon our organizational needs and constraints. We must consider the services we offer, the customer experience we want to deliver, the breadth and depth of expertise we require, and the economics of our situation. It seems safe to say that in most cases, some number of generalists are required if customer interaction or broad problem solving is needed. This is also vital to succession planning, as leaders must often be generalists, with a big-picture view of the situation.

We must also consider the individual strengths required for optimal success. This goes beyond our traditional searches for skills and knowledge that are directly applicable to the job. Instead, it implies some natural trait—or group of traits—that fit specific roles and generally help address gaps in the team.

In his book *The Ten Faces of Innovation*, Tom Kelley, co-founder of the award-winning design firm IDEO, suggests we consider which personas we may need on our team. He offers ten personas for creative teams. That is not to say that each person on the team needs to encompass all ten, nor is it necessary to have all ten personas represented on the team. They should all be considered, however, and the ones that apply to our situation should be covered somehow. The personas Kelley offers are as follows (I've paraphrased the descriptions):

Persona	Description
1. The Anthropologist	Observes the customer and empathizes to determine what's really needed
2. The Experimenter	Not afraid to try new avenues using a "fail fast, fail cheap" mentality
3. The Cross-Pollinator	Examines multiple industries, genres, and cultures to mine for ideas and look for inspiration
4. The Hurdler	Bends the rules to get around roadblocks, undeterred by adversity; gets the job done
5. The Collaborator	Brings diverse groups together, even when leading from the middle of the pack; partners with people to provide solutions
6. The Director	Assembles the right people and creates an environment for success; sets the right theme
7. The Experience Architect	Designs a unique and creative customer experience beyond just the functionality of the product

Persona	Description
8. The Set Designer	Creates a fun and vibrant physical working environment that can spark creativity and collaboration
9. The Caregiver	Anticipates customer needs before, during, and after the engagement, and goes above and beyond normal expectations
10. The Storyteller	Builds internal morale and external awareness through compelling stories and case studies that reinforce key values or traits

[11]

Some of these may not apply to every organization or team, but they are well worth considering. Aside from the personas, Kelley goes on to say that IDEO often searches for "T-Shaped people," those who have a strong foundation in one or two areas of knowledge, but a general interest in many areas.[12] This could also equate to what one might call a "Specialized Generalist" or "Generalized Specialist," someone who has deep expertise in one or two domains but has a broad base of knowledge. This can create the ultimate in flexibility, provided that the person doesn't get tied up in the weeds too frequently to be an effective generalist.

We shouldn't hesitate to be creative when filling a position. For example, when the theft-damaged Edvard Munch masterpieces *The Scream* and *Madonna* needed particles of glass removed during their restoration, the director of the Munch Museum in Norway, Lise Mjoes, didn't search for the most skilled artist to do the work. Instead, she searched for someone with the talent and equipment for the delicate removal of fine pieces of glass. She sought an eye surgeon for the work.[13]

In our never-ending search to find effective methods of resource management and staffing, let's not forget that resources are people, too. And people have likes, dislikes, and breaking points. On one hand, we want to make full use of people's talents, but on the other hand, we don't want to stretch our people too thin. In addition, we need to be aware of their working preferences, as some people prefer variety and others prefer focused discipline. Also, staffing a team is not about fitting pegs into holes. Each individual we choose will bring unique talents to the team that can create unexpected value.

Most of all, we need to have realistic expectations and not assume people can have breadth and depth and be effective as both generalists and specialists.

Consider the plight of CEOs. James Citrin, an executive recruiter, has placed nearly 200 senior executives, including some of the top CEOs in the business. He sees what works and what doesn't. According to Citrin, organizations are mistakenly expecting CEOs to be able to be masters of all trades. In a recent *Business Week* article, he claims:

> *Boards of directors will need to get more realistic about the rarity of the perfect CEO. Rather than holding out for leaders who are expert at everything, they should instead warm up to CEOs with deep expertise in one or two crucial areas and enough know-how in the rest to build a high-performing supporting cast.[14]*

Robert Heinlein once wrote:

> *A human being should be able to change a diaper, plan an invasion, butcher a hog, conn a ship, design a building, write a sonnet, balance accounts, build a wall, set a bone, comfort*

*the dying, take orders, give orders, cooperate, act alone, solve
equations, analyze a new problem, pitch manure, program a
computer, cook a tasty meal, fight efficiently and die gallantly.
Specialization is for insects.*

While this may be true—in that not even the most
focused specialist truly knows only one area—it would be
awfully difficult to do all of these things effectively, and
certainly difficult to do them all at the same time.

Unfortunately, Heinlein's statement of superhuman
capability is the equivalent of what some organizations expect from their people. Instead, we need to consider many
factors, such as:

- Where we need deep expertise and where we might
  need broad problem solving
- The need for analysis, customer focus, and
  negotiation skills
- The volume of work that flows into the department
- Where we might need leadership traits, now and in
  the future

With these considerations, we can begin to assemble
a team.

In addition, as Marcus Buckingham and Curt Coffman
suggest, we should consider having growth paths of
prestige within a specialty area and not promote people
to management solely because of tenure or expertise in
their chosen specialty.[15] Leaders, much like generalists on
the whole, require certain traits. Tom Peters notes in his
presentations that orchestras don't automatically promote
the first violinist to conductor after a certain number of
years, and businesses shouldn't follow this practice either.
Yet they often do.

Indeed, there is much to think about when staffing and maintaining a team. And as more companies become decentralized, with specialists distributed across multiple departments, these considerations are even more vital. Undoubtedly, leveraging generalists and specialists is an art more than it is a science; thus, it is one of our gray areas.

Key Concepts

- Generalists are able to integrate knowledge from a wide variety of sources, giving them a better sense of the big picture. Because of their broad exposure, generalists are often able to offer creative solutions and are best equipped to perform initial diagnoses of problems.

- Generalists who excel at communication and negotiation are most often targeted for leadership.

- Generalists cannot always afford to dive in too deep in any one area, as their performance can suffer if they get dragged into a particular activity at the expense of their other duties.

- Generalists may sometimes oversimplify theories and miss crucial particulars about a problem.

- Specialists are able to gain deep expertise through repetition and concentration.

- Specialists excel at identifying and implementing solutions, but they are not in an ideal position for performing initial diagnoses.

- Specialists don't always communicate well with others and may sometimes ignore or discredit areas outside of their domain.

- Specialists may sometimes frame solutions solely based on their area of expertise.

- Generalists and specialists who work together repeatedly build rapport, which is vital to avoiding communication breakdowns.

- A handoff checklist, requiring a telephone conversation for all initial handoffs, and having a generalist serve to coordinate all handoffs for a particular problem can help to better manage handoffs.

- Gordon Rugg's Verifier Approach, as described in this chapter, is useful to validate gaps in thinking caused by narrow focus and disjointed efforts.

- Achieving the right balance of generalists and specialists when staffing a team depends upon organizational needs, the breadth and depth of expertise required, and the volume of work that flows into the area.

- Staffing a team is not about fitting pegs into holes. Each individual will bring unique value to the team that may lead to unexpected benefits.

- Most people cannot be effective as both a specialist and a generalist; it is difficult to maintain both broad and deep expertise. Yet a generalist with knowledge of one or two specialty areas can be a valuable asset.

? Questions to Ponder

1. Does the nature of the work on my team require a high degree of interaction, either with customers or with other team members?

2. What roles on my team require strong depth of expertise? Can I afford to staff with generalists for most of the work, and leverage specialists from other teams or from outside of the organization as needed? Or do some areas require including specialists on the team?

3. Do I have people on my team with the breadth of knowledge, systems-thinking ability, and communication skills for initial problem solving and problem routing? If not, how can I build or obtain that skill on my team?

4. How might I rearrange my team, or the entire organization, to build rapport between people who need to work together to solve problems?

5. Am I aware of each team member's strengths, weaknesses, likes, and dislikes? Have I balanced their work assignments accordingly?

Notes

Get even more from this book. Visit **www.rmcpublications.com/grayareas** to share your thoughts and questions on topics in this chapter and to access additional resources.

Chapter 5
Big Picture vs. Narrow Focus

"The single biggest problem in communication is the illusion that it has taken place."

\- George Bernard Shaw

Fundamental Question:
How much detail should I share with my team?

Do people always need to see the big picture? At first glance, it would seem that anyone could benefit from understanding his or her job in the context of the greater picture. Consider this popular anecdote Peter Drucker relays in his book *Management: Tasks, Responsibilities, Practices*:

> *An old story tells of three stonecutters who were asked what they were doing. The first replied, "I am making a living." The second kept on hammering while he said, "I am doing the best job of stonecutting in the entire country." The third one looked up with a visionary gleam in his eyes and said, "I am building a cathedral."* [1]

Drucker notes that the first stonecutter will typically give an adequate effort for a day's wages. The third stonecutter is a leader or manager (or at least has potential to be), with a keen eye toward the big picture. Drucker cautions that the second stonecutter, the one who is focused on doing the best job in the entire country, could be the most troublesome if he's not adequately tuned in to the overall goal. He *thinks* he's performing excellent work, when in reality he could be way off base.

This anecdote promotes the theory that if people understand why something is being done, they will more likely meet the requirements of their task, have higher morale, and be in a better position to act independently if needed. In most cases, this is true. However, some situations may cause us to think twice about whether it makes sense to share the full vision. For example, we may not have fleshed out the long-term vision yet, and thus wouldn't want to bombard people with incomplete information. In some extreme cases, security or exact accuracy may be required, and there may be specific rules which must be precisely adhered to.

Indeed, whether to share the big picture is not quite as straightforward as it may seem. Leaders need to consider the situation, the individuals involved, and the nature of the information being shared. Ultimately, there are two factors we must consider when striving for the engagement of our team while communicating: *simplicity* and *context*. Let's examine each in more detail.

Simplicity

A long-held axiom of communication is that it is best to break complex messages into simple chunks, issued in a piecemeal fashion. Marketing experts use this approach. For any given product, they'll typically initiate one marketing campaign at a time, with a catchy tag line that they hope will capture the attention of an increasingly distracted public. Leaders are taught this as well, as complex messages tend to get lost in the shuffle. When Napoleon took over France following the chaos of the French Revolution, he didn't bombard the public with all of his plans and future initiatives. He addressed one issue at a time, first announcing the preparation of a constitution, then addressing financial reforms, then education reforms, and so on. Whatever the issue was at the time became the overarching theme of his administration.

Today's political campaigns follow a similar approach, by adopting a major theme and creating in the minds of the public an association between that theme and the political candidate. It is likely that this theme does not represent the big picture but is merely one of many ideas the candidate has in store. In essence, the theme is the short-range vision. It is something everyone can grasp.

With young children, experts suggest that we avoid providing a full explanation when answering their questions. Often, partial information is appropriate for their needs and too much information can open Pandora's Box. As children mature, we can provide more comprehensive answers. Most adults, however, are able to comprehend, and in fact need to know, the context in which they are operating. Does this conflict with the view that simple, piecemeal messages can provide clarity? Not necessarily. It's a matter of addressing two needs: *people's need to have simple, digestible messages to focus on* and *their need to understand why they're being asked to do something or to embrace something.* Put simply, we must endeavor to address both simplicity and context whenever we communicate.

Context

There is no formula for integrating simplicity and context. But there are some general guidelines we can use. If the short-range vision is a singular one, with perhaps two or three supporting goals, then it is likely digestible enough to address the first factor—simplicity. If this vision is compelling on its own, independent of the long-range vision, then it will likely satisfy the second factor as well—context. If the short-range vision is merely a stepping stone toward the long-range vision and is not compelling as a stand-alone initiative, then it will likely be necessary to also share some elements of the long-range vision. It is often helpful for people to see a high-level roadmap, which provides greater context and yet doesn't distract from the short-range vision.

There are, of course, exceptions, such as when dealing with sensitive information that must remain private or when work must be done to a certain specification without variation. Even in the military, however, where information is often filtered for security reasons and soldiers are frequently given specific orders, things are changing. Military leaders are slowly catching on, as are enlightened business leaders, that there are great benefits to enabling and fostering situational awareness. Situational awareness enables people to leverage knowledge of the political and physical environment in which they are working. Armed with such knowledge, they can better understand the potential implications of their actions and make better decisions. Situational awareness is the ultimate in context.

In a government-sponsored research report for the U.S. Department of Defense, *Command Concepts: A Theory Derived from the Practice of Command and Control*, authors Carl Builder, Steven Bankes, and Richard Nordin suggest that, prior to any military engagement, leaders convey to their troops the full context of the mission—what the authors call the *command concept*. For a large initiative with multiple tiers of organizational hierarchy, there may be lower levels in the hierarchy with concepts that tie back to higher-level command concepts. While it is important that the concept at each level is relevant to that team and does not contain extraneous details, it is equally important to include the tie-back to the overall command concept.[2] Once again, we must integrate simplicity and context.

Ideally, a command concept should include the context in which it was developed. At the very least, it should state the following:

- The problem or opportunity to be addressed
- The expected outcomes/objectives to be met
- A realistic timeline
- Information about the physical and organizational environment in which the team will be working
- What to expect from unfolding events (i.e., risk awareness)
- Communication protocols
- Contingencies, should something go wrong

This information enables those in the field to be more engaged and puts them in a better position to react to changing circumstances and unexpected events. It also reduces the chance for error and allows for subsequent communication to be concise and exception-based. Since everyone understands the context of the mission and the operating principles, one only need ask if anything has changed that will impact the desired outcomes or if anything new is needed. Perhaps most importantly, an engaged, connected, and alert team is able to report back relevant updates to management and even suggest changes to the command concept. Leadership becomes a two-way street.

The command concept approach, along with the accompanying bilateral communication, is relevant in business as well as in the military. In a recent survey of nearly two thousand professionals conducted by Dr. Joanne Sujansky's KEYGroup Consulting, more than half of the respondents agreed with or were neutral to the statement that their management is disconnected from daily business activity. In addition, nearly half of those surveyed stated that their job goals are unclear.[3]

As organizations grow and become more complex, these issues are only getting worse. It becomes difficult to find the forest for the trees in an organization that has grown through mergers, diversified into a cornucopia of business lines, or added layer upon layer of management. Regardless of the organization's size, it doesn't help that organizational leaders often assume that everyone is on the same page and that everyone understands the organization's goals. As Sujansky reports, employees may understand the tasks they've been assigned, but they have trouble connecting those tasks to the big picture.[4] Likewise, managers are removed from the daily details faced by their employees. Thus, we often have managers and employees operating on different planes.

The uninspiring words of most mission statements don't help the situation any either. Sujansky references the Dilbert Web site's "Mission Statement Generator" (http://www.dilbert.com/comics/dilbert/games/index.html), which I must say I've occasionally visited for a laugh. Sadly, the results look like most organizations' mission statements. It's no wonder employees don't feel engaged.

Engagement

We have explored the need to address both simplicity and context when communicating. But we cannot expect that communicating at the same level to everyone will have the same impact on each person, nor will communication guarantee engagement. Nowhere is this more evident than when organizations announce a mission statement or vision statement and assume that the announcement alone will magically align everyone with the organization's goals. The idea that an announcement will not guarantee engagement is true no matter how compelling the mission statement may seem. As motivational expert Tony Robbins says, "To effectively communicate, we must realize that we are all different in the way we perceive the world and use this understanding as a guide to our communication with others."

Thus, to increase engagement, we must understand the various motivating factors involved. There are benefits to directing people's attention to incremental challenges as well as to presenting the big picture. Striving for incremental challenges not only achieves simplicity, but it allows for faster feedback as well, which in turn serves to motivate people for the next hurdle. Knowing the big picture also helps, in that it gives added meaning to each successive accomplishment and thus provides the context we seek.

Noted CEO and author Jack Stack wrote a book called *The Great Game of Business*, as well as a follow-up called *A Stake in the Outcome*. In both books, he encourages what he calls open-book management and the concept of creating a culture of ownership. The premise is that, with knowledge and awareness, people tend to feel more engaged and accountable. Stack's assertion is that education breeds engagement and enables a more democratic work environment—which in turn breeds even more engagement. As Stack says of his people:

> *I want to give them a game plan that allows them to make their own decisions. I want them to see how their decisions fit into the overall puzzle. So you have to educate them first. Without education, you don't have democracy. All you have is manipulation. There is no democratic process if people don't have any idea what you're talking about.* [5]

If our vision hasn't been well thought-out and needs to evolve over time, we may not want to alarm people unnecessarily by communicating a vision prematurely. Consider the words of Cyrus the Great, who founded the Persian Empire twenty-five hundred years ago. (His legacy is that he later became equally regarded by Jews, Muslims, and Christians as the wisest and fairest of leaders—not a small feat.)

I paused, wanting to prophesy about the new world that I was now setting into motion. I checked myself, however, feeling it unwise to announce the beginning of a campaign of unprecedented scope. In the coming months I would force myself again and again to guard against my own overeagerness... The full extent of my plans would gradually be unfolded to my officers. To shock them with the whole truth at the beginning would cause too many of them to shy away. It would also lead to accusations that I was working to overthrow our present form of government, and that was the last alarm I wanted to sound.[6]

We must also realize that communicating a long-term vision is not a guarantee of engagement. Some people may be more concerned about what's in it for them personally, either materially or emotionally. They may feel detached unless there clearly is something in it for them. Therefore, we must be cognizant of their interests.

One way to make even the skeptics feel engaged is to ask for help. Years ago, I worked for a man named Herb Vincent. I was in charge of the education program for a national IBM business partner, and Herb, a former IBM executive, was the director of the Philadelphia branch. Each week, Herb would gather everyone in the branch, regardless of position, for a meeting. He'd ask everyone for input on how to make the branch the best one in the organization. He'd raise the most pressing issues at the time and ask for our help. He'd ask for input on business ideas as well. As a result, many of us felt a sense of ownership in the company. There may have been those who didn't appreciate this approach and who would have been more motivated by direct personal gain or by having specific tasks to accomplish. But for many, simply being asked for help and being listened to was refreshing.

Indeed, spoon-feeding orders to our team inhibits learning and growth. Where possible, it is usually better to provide information about the need or situation and challenge people to solve problems on their own. In the end, much depends on the circumstances, the individuals involved, the complexity of the information, and a dozen other factors. Generally, if we communicate with simplicity and context, with an understanding of people's motivating factors, we'll be much better equipped to field an engaged team.

Key Concepts

- In addressing simplicity and context, we are meeting two needs: the need for people to have simple, digestible messages to focus on, and the need for them to understand why they're being asked to do something or embrace something.

- Whether a message must be tied to a long-range vision depends on how well thought-out the long-range vision is and whether the short-range vision is compelling and understandable in itself.

- Sometimes a high-level roadmap can provide beneficial glimpses of the long-range vision without causing distraction.

- There are times when it may be best not to share a long-range vision, for example if it hasn't been well thought-out yet and would thus raise concerns unnecessarily.

- Communicating the entire concept of the current mission, including the problem or opportunity, expected outcome, objectives, a realistic timeline, organizational advice, what to expect from unfolding events, communication protocols, and contingencies should something go wrong, provides the ultimate in context.

- We cannot expect that communicating in the same way to everyone will have the same impact on each person. We must understand the various motivating factors involved.

- For most people, understanding the big picture serves as motivation. Yet there are some who would prefer to focus on the immediate task at hand and/or what will bring them personal gain. We must be cognizant of their interests.

- Asking for help usually engages people, as most people simply want to feel needed.

? Questions to Ponder

1. Do I unwittingly keep people on my team in the dark? What can I do to communicate more effectively to everyone?

2. Do I typically provide a few major goals that my team can rally around, or do I communicate so many topics that they all get lost in the shuffle?

3. Do I communicate a major initiative or vision and assume that everyone will feel as compelled by it as I do? What are some ways people may react that I haven't considered?

4. Are my messages usually framed with both simplicity and context, or am I lacking either of these elements? What can I do differently?

5. Do I ever ask my team for help, or do I simply issue directives? Are there areas where engaging them in cocreating a solution to a common problem would minimize resistance?

 Notes

Get even more from this book. Visit **www.rmcpublications.com/grayareas** to share your thoughts and questions on topics in this chapter and to access additional resources.

Chapter 6
Structure vs. Flexibility

"A great man knows when to yield and when not."
- Chinese proverb

Fundamental Question:

How can I maintain a sense of order without compromising productivity?

Structure, including derivatives such as process, methodology, hierarchy, standards, rules, and systems, is often seen as a way to promote consistent success. But when overused or misapplied, it can stifle productivity and render us unprepared to deal with natural variability in workplace activities. To aid us in determining the right level of structure for our systems, we can once again learn much from nature, which is itself a beautiful mélange of organization and chance—of strength and pliability. Consider the leaderless, yet structured, routine of insects, birds, and other social creatures, or the strong, yet flexible, makeup of a leaf. Consider also the concept of *entropy*, which is a measure of the level of disorder in a system (and thus energy spent). Although disorder is a necessary component of progress, disorder can quickly change into chaos if there's no constraining force. Yet if there's too much control, we cannot leverage the energy that disorder brings about.

Indeed, what we must do is embrace both order and disorder. It seems that organizations everywhere cling to structure to the detriment of productivity. If we define productivity as the amount and frequency of valuable output created (the operative word being *valuable*), the need to embrace both order and disorder becomes evident. Most output is produced through disorder, provided the disorder is channeled in the right direction through some constraining force or structure. If we apply too much—or the wrong type of—direction, we hurt productivity. Let's look at some typical examples of this.

Structure Misused

Structure can be a wonderful thing. In fact, it is necessary in order to provide a proper foundation for correct action. It can also help with consistency where consistency is needed. But many organizations apply structure unilaterally and arbitrarily. Consider those who embrace a rigid, all-purpose project management methodology. Not every process step is required for all projects, and certainly not at the same level of rigor. One project may benefit from a big design up front (commonly known as BDUF), while another may be better off with adapting incrementally, based on feedback from prototypes and pilots. One project may require a ten-page business case, while another may only need a one-page justification. When a rigid methodology is mandated, the organization typically resists, realizing that the methodology doesn't apply to all situations. They call for the abolishment of the department that created it (usually the Program Management Office, or PMO), claiming that it slows things down and doesn't add value, and the baby is thrown out with the bath water.

Likewise, organizations often implement rigid change policies that require all changes to follow the same obstacle course to approval, regardless of the size or potential impact of the change. This can apply to project changes, software changes, policy changes, or any other type of change. Some changes require rigorous management. Others do not. In the end, excessive roadblocks, bureaucracy, and approval requirements lead to delay, frustration, and eventually apathy. Trying to get anything accomplished becomes like the 12 trials of Hercules.

Another way organizations misapply structure is when they adopt popular solutions in an arbitrary manner. For example, Six Sigma, which began at Motorola and was popularized by Jack Welch's GE organization, is meant to improve or fix existing processes. Put simply, it's a quality improvement tool to reduce defects, using a basic framework called DMAIC (Define, Measure, Analyze, Improve, Control). Many people apply it generically to all of their efforts. While certain elements of Six Sigma, such as its focus on identifying prioritized needs and Critical-to-Quality (CTQ) elements, may apply more broadly, that doesn't mean the whole framework applies universally. Sometimes, broader or more systemic changes are needed, and applying incremental fixes, such as those Six Sigma seeks to address, is not appropriate.

Organizations run into the same trouble with Business Process Reengineering (BPR), popularized by Michael Hammer and James Champy in their landmark book *Reengineering the Corporation*. BPR is meant to recreate an entire end-to-end business process from scratch, making the assumption that the old technology and old business model are obsolete. Its focus is on meeting customer needs through a new business model, rather than through improving existing systems. BPR begins by examining the "as-is" state of the organization's end-to-end processes. It then creates a "to-be" state using input from best practices, modeling, interviews, and brainstorming. Lastly, it addresses gaps between the "as-is" and "to-be" states, including necessary technology. In some cases, this clean-slate approach is a creative way to embrace a new paradigm and take an organization into the future (or at least into the present).[1] Yet in many cases, such a major overhaul is unnecessary, and simple adjustments will suffice.

A frequent byproduct of reengineering is the need for less staff, due to reduction in redundancies and handoffs. Unfortunately, many organizations seized this as an opportunity to cut costs and began undertaking huge BPR initiatives with the wrong focus. Reengineering became synonymous with downsizing, which was not the intention of its creators. And, because the organizations focused on cutting costs more than satisfying customers, the effort did not result in value. Key resources were let go, and business models didn't take customer needs into account. Thus, efficiency was achieved, but productivity, which, if you recall, requires valuable output, was not.

For their book on evidence-based management, Jeffrey Pfeffer and Bob Sutton studied countless organizations that had undertaken major change, including Enterprise Resource Planning (ERP) implementations, Six Sigma programs, BPR, cost-cutting initiatives, and other such endeavors. The evidence showed that these initiatives frequently carry risks that outweigh the benefits and that they are commonly misapplied. People tend to underestimate the costs and overestimate the gains, and the only ones who consistently benefit are the consultants.[2]

Perhaps Peter Drucker put it best when he wrote, "There is surely nothing quite so useless as doing with great efficiency what should not be done at all."

Integrating Structure and Flexibility

We've discussed how applying too much structure, such as a universal project management methodology or a rigid change process, can lead to frustration and apathy. We've also discussed how the wrong type of structure, such as the misapplication of Six Sigma or BPR, can waste time and money. When structure is applied correctly and appropriately, it provides much-needed order and consistency and allows for proven methods to be leveraged. Implementing standards is a method commonly used by organizations to impose structure. However, having standards does not necessarily mean impeding creativity and engagement. In fact, we can engage people and energize them by asking for their help in creating and refining standards. We can also engage people in using continuous improvement methods to enhance those standards even further over time.

Standardization is *everyone's* job. If we impose standards from the top, we alienate people. Consider the insights of Peter Scholtes, one of the world's foremost authorities on quality:

> There is a delicate line to walk when dealing with standardization. On the one hand, we want methods of work that are usefully constraining, that eliminate needless variation in method, and, therefore, in output...While we want to eliminate art-form-like caprice and needless variation from work, we do not want to make work oppressively rigid and obnoxiously bureaucratic. Between these is the fine line. By involving people in the standardization of work, we can remove some of the oppressiveness of it. People are less likely to balk at standards they have devised. Recognizing that we need not standardize everything should help. Also, agreeing to begin with those processes that we all acknowledge need standardization

should help. The ideal is for people to take charge of their own standardization effort.[3]

To be successful, we need to integrate structure with flexibility. We need to create what is known as a *chaordic* organization.

Chaordic (a term coined by leadership guru and former Visa CEO Dee Hock, and made up from the words *chaos* and *order*) refers to a state in which systems (and life) "thrive on the edge of chaos with just enough order to give them pattern, but not so much to slow their adaptation and learning."[4] In a chaordic organization, neither hierarchy nor anarchy rules the roost. Garry Booker, whose organization Project Frontier specializes in innovative project management research, refers to this as "top-down control and bottom-up chaos." Booker suggests we first accept that there are two independent, yet connected, realms—*outcomes* and *actions*—and they should be managed in different ways. Managers must control desired outcomes in a structured manner and let their teams generate and manage the correct actions that support the outcomes.

It is worth noting that outcomes are not the same as deliverables. Outcomes may include deliverables, but they also include meeting nonfunctional requirements (such as safety, usability, performance, etc.), satisfying customer expectations, and achieving other organizational goals. In other words, outcomes represent true value. In fact, any time someone wants to introduce a structured process, it's a good idea to ask, "What are the intended outcomes?" You may find that there are much simpler and less invasive ways of achieving the same outcomes than what is being proposed.

Let's examine the concept of chaordism from the project management perspective. Booker defines a project as "a set of actions that are focused on an established set of outcomes." This is a perfect definition, as it raises awareness of the need to define and focus on outcomes. As Booker suggests, the outcomes represent the direction, much like the rudder of a ship, and the actions represent propulsion, much like the engine or the oars. We must tightly manage any changes to the intended outcomes (i.e., the agreed-upon scope of the project) while at the same time giving our team members the freedom to control their own actions that support the outcomes, within reason of course. This also enables the team members to agree on which standards to apply to their project. Allowing this flexibility puts the more detailed planning in the hands of those closest to the action, who then contribute feedback to the master plan (and recommend changes to the standard tool set as needed). Thus, we have both top-down and bottom-up planning—structure and flexibility.

Some actions, such as those that must meet regulatory or safety requirements or those that must adhere to exact specifications, cannot afford flexibility. Those are the exceptions.

The very fact that we're dealing with human beings adds a level of complexity into the mix. This is the reason cybernetic models, which operate on algorithms and feedback loops, cannot completely imitate human behavior when it comes to complex jobs.[5] Only that which is predictable can be modeled. A cybernetic system could not, for example, duplicate the insights of a great leader or act on a random discovery during a hallway meeting or an e-mail exchange. It could not conceive of the occasional alterations that may be needed as situations change or better methods are found. And it could not replicate the contributions of a seasoned subject matter expert. This is chaos at its best, and it is how most work gets done on projects.

In a chaordic organization that integrates structure and flexibility, team members are like volunteers.[6] They act of their own accord to work in line with outcomes that the leader has convinced them are valuable (for a large endeavor, it may be beneficial to have subleaders, responsible for managing the outcomes for their respective areas).

The leader's primary purpose, then, is to inspire others to support outcomes that are in line with the organization's goals. This takes both structure and flexibility: structure to ensure the outcomes are managed, and flexibility to let people set their own actions. In Chapter 7, we will see examples of organizations that have achieved this chaordic state.

Time Management and Flexibility

Another area in which structure must be integrated with flexibility is time management. This includes managing your own time and managing other people's time. In both cases, the same principles apply. Among the common dilemmas that many leaders face are: *How do I manage my own time, yet remain available to my staff?* and *How do I ensure that my team maintains adequate process discipline, yet is adaptable to customer needs?*

Consider the instructions a flight attendant gives at the beginning of any flight: *In case of emergency, if you're traveling with a small child, give yourself oxygen first.* The same holds true whether you're supporting your team or your team is supporting its customers. In order to be effective, you must first secure stability for yourself. Then—and only then—will you be able to serve others.

Inevitably, emergencies arise. Team members reach a barrier and cannot proceed until they speak with you. Customers have a pressing need that may justify bypassing your usual schedule. But these exceptions do not automatically negate the need to have some time put aside for yourself and your team.

Mihaly Csikszentmihalyi, renowned psychology professor, author, and creator of the concept of *flow*, notes that constant interruptions to you or your team can break concentration and disrupt productivity.[7] This has only gotten worse with the advent of e-mail, smart phones, and other modern forms of interruption. Blocks of time need to be put aside for concentration and reflection, and guidelines must be established to allow for exceptions. Csikszentmihalyi offers the following sage advice:

> *The manager who does not put some time aside for reflection every day is likely to be headed for burnout. And the manager who does not actively protect his subordinates' psychic energy from being disrupted is going to have a frustrated staff. It takes trust to respect a closed door, or private space in the maze of cubbyholes; but the manager who encourages workers to set a "Do Not Disturb" policy when necessary is not likely to regret it.*[8]

We must heed the words *when necessary* in Csikszentmihalyi's last sentence. Some people take an extreme approach and go into hibernation, only coming out of their office for lunch or to go to meetings. We need to balance private time and availability.

This same concept applies regarding availability to our customers. According to Marcus Buckingham and Curt Coffman, customers have four primary needs. The most basic needs are *accuracy* and *availability*, in that order. With those needs satisfied, the next successive needs are *partnership* and *advice*.[9] Think of the basic needs of accuracy and availability in terms of Herzberg's hygiene factors, which we discussed in Chapter 3. They are not motivators in themselves, but they are dissatisfiers if they are not present.

We can best satisfy accuracy and availability—not just for one customer, but for our customer base as a whole—by "giving ourselves oxygen first" and ensuring we have adequate structures in place. An often-overlooked method of improving accuracy and availability is to have adequate governance processes, including prioritization and some sort of intake filter, in order to focus our people on the most important work. One of the most common complaints among workers is that their organization "opens the floodgates," requiring them to take on too much activity at once. In doing this, we cause burnout and mistakes, we disrupt people's flow of concentration, and ultimately, we cause *everything* to take longer. A classic case of this is an organization that has hundreds of active projects, but none of them are getting completed. In overloading our people, we also deny them the opportunity to observe adequate process discipline for those items that require such discipline.

By looking at the organization as a holistic system, we can better see how such damage can be caused and take steps to avoid it. We will explore systems thinking in more detail in Chapter 10.

If we throw structure to the wind in order to satisfy one customer, we run the risk of decreasing accuracy and/or availability for our other customers. We can prevent the necessary rigor from impacting customers by promoting a customer-centric culture and proactively communicating with our customers. Thus, we give a better perception of availability and set the stage for partnership and advice. There is an additional gray area to consider here: Should we provide the same level of accuracy and availability to all of our customers, or should we offer a hierarchy of service levels? In other words, should all customers be considered equal? There is no prescriptive solution to this, other than the caution that wounded enemies can come back to bite us later. If multiple levels of service are provided, it is usually better to offer a choice to the customer.

We must also consider structure and flexibility when dealing with customers' requests for changes. With no structure at all, our time will be spent chasing rainbows, as customers demand more and more. When developing a product for a customer, it is advisable to allow a certain number of feedback loops to give the customer ample opportunity to suggest changes. Software developers do this all the time. They employ rapid prototypes and/or piecemeal delivery of the product, allowing the customer to suggest changes each time. After a predetermined number of iterations, they publish a release. Subsequent changes can be delivered in the next release, and so on. This method is good way to remain adaptive, yet provide enough structure to prevent chaos.

When implementing governance and prioritization processes, we must avoid creating so rigid a structure that creativity and boldness are stifled. Thus, we should allow room for experimental projects as well, perhaps dedicating certain individuals to them. This is where a balance between structure and flexibility is needed. Much like a balanced financial portfolio, an organization needs to determine the amount of high-risk/potential high-payback projects it can endure, keeping in mind that competitors are out there taking risks.

Strategy and Flexibility

Strategy is yet another form of structure that we must blend with flexibility. Some organizations have a strategic hierarchy, whereby the top executives set the strategy for the year and each department creates plans that support the strategy. Then everyone allegedly marches in line. To those organizations, it would seem heretical to propose the reverse scenario, in which random ideas, experimentation, and feedback from employees and customers create strategy. Yet many successful organizations do just that. For their studies on evidence-based management, Pfeffer and Sutton interviewed John Sall, one of the cofounders of SAS Institute, the world's largest privately owned software company. In the interview, Sall noted that Stanford University is very particular about selecting students for their two-year MBA program. He questioned, "Why should it take two years to teach such smart people the secret to success; listen to your customers, listen to your employees, do what they tell you?"[10]

Pfeffer and Sutton also cite eBay's CEO, Meg Whitman, who stated that eBay was successful mainly because of its focus on experimentation and learning over heavy strategic planning. To this, Whitman added that it's faster to release something, see if it works, and make changes, than it is to wait until the perfect strategy is in place.[11] As General Patton once said, "A good plan today is better than a perfect plan tomorrow."

Tom Kelley of IDEO calls this iterative approach "enlightened trial and error," which, in essence, is the ability to create a reasonable theory, try it out, and use lessons learned to make adjustments. Is this the equivalent of "winging it"? Indeed it is not, as it takes a deliberate process to conceive of the right ideas to begin with, as well as to implement a progressive learning approach. Additionally, it takes structure to focus on learning and practicing effective operations, which is where most projects succeed or fail. Creating a strategy is not a bad thing to do. Focusing on strategy at the expense of execution and learning is.

 **Key Concepts**

- To be successful, we need a combination of structure and flexibility—order and disorder.

- Most output is produced through disorder, provided the disorder is channeled in the right direction through some constraining force or structure.

- Structure is frequently misapplied or applied arbitrarily. Examples include a rigid, all-purpose project management methodology that assumes all projects require the same amount of rigor, or the application of structured processes, such as Six Sigma and Business Process Reengineering (BPR), for reasons other than their intended purpose.

- We can achieve a chaordic organization (one that combines chaos and disorder, as coined by Dee Hock) by separating outcomes from actions. Managers must control outcomes in a structured manner, and let their team generate and manage the correct actions that support the outcomes, where appropriate.

- Outcomes are not the same as deliverables. Outcomes may *include* deliverables, but they also include meeting nonfunctional requirements (such as safety, usability, performance needs, etc.), satisfying customer expectations, and achieving other organizational goals.

- Having standards does not mean impeding creativity and engagement. On the contrary, standards work best when they are defined and maintained from the bottom up, rather than imposed from the top down.

- To be effective, we must first secure stability for ourselves. Then—and only then—will we be able to serve others. Blocks of time should be put aside for concentration and reflection, and guidelines must be established to allow for exceptions.

- If we "open the floodgates," requiring people to take on too much activity at once, we cause burnout and mistakes, we disrupt people's flow, and ultimately, we cause *everything* to take longer. We need good governance processes to avoid this, including prioritization and some sort of filtering process.

- Strategy is yet another form of structure that we must blend with flexibility. It is often faster to try something, see if it works, and make changes, than it is to wait until the perfect strategy is in place.

? Questions to Ponder

1. In what ways can I focus more on managing outcomes and let my team have more control over the supporting actions?

2. Is there room in my organization for experimentation?

3. Do I make time for myself and encourage my team to arrange for "quiet time" as well?

4. Do I make sure I am frequently available to my team and my customers?

5. Do my team's processes allow for adjustments based on customer involvement and feedback?

6. What operations can my team improve upon that would make them more effective?

Notes

Get even more from this book. Visit **www.rmcpublications.com/grayareas** to share your thoughts and questions on topics in this chapter and to access additional resources.

Chapter 7
Vigilance vs. Delegation

"Never tell people how to do things. Tell them what to do and they will surprise you with their ingenuity."
- George S. Patton

Fundamental Question:

How much can I trust the people on my team to do what they're supposed to do? Where should accountability lie?

Managers are taught to be vigilant, ensuring that no detail is overlooked. Yet in many cases, this vigilance leads to micromanagement, putting accountability in the hands of the manager and not the staff doing the work. At the other extreme, there are "hands-off" managers who delegate everything to their staff, providing no guidance whatsoever. Such managers might want to heed Robert Half's observation, "Delegating works, provided the one delegating works, too."

Delegation is not an "all or nothing" proposition. Often a mix is warranted, using appropriate levels of delegation depending on the individuals' level of expertise or when certain specifications must be met. In most cases, people will flourish if they are provided with guiding principles, realistic objectives, and the means to achieve those objectives. Freedom tends to breed accountability. Generally, by "doing for" and "telling how," we rob people of the ability to assume full responsibility for their outcomes and to achieve great things. Ultimately, we damage their self-esteem as well. What is needed is a way to combine adequate vigilance with the right levels of delegation and coaching—and knowledge of when and how to provide supportive versus directive leadership.

Freedom and Accountability

Child psychologist Saul Fisher suggests that parents recognize three enablers for instilling self-esteem in their children:

1. Positive connection
2. Competency through achievement
3. Specific (not general) feedback

In supporting this, he recommends that parents consider three general principles:

1. Don't "do for"
2. Encourage a "can-do" attitude
3. Always set clear expectations and outcomes

For setting and meeting expectations and outcomes, Fisher suggests holding family meetings to solicit the child's input. Finally, in keeping with the rule of three, he suggests that there are three kinds of parents:

1. Jellyfish: Those who have no structure whatsoever
2. Steel Rods: Those who are unbendable
3. Backbones: Those who are supportive and flexible, yet provide adequate structure

To foster self-esteem, it is, of course, most effective to be the latter.

While it would be a mistake to assume that the rules of parenting always apply to management, these basic principles of self-esteem are as valid for adults as they are for children. We need to develop a positive connection with our employees, let them undertake actions and learn from mistakes, and provide specific outcomes that are in line with organizational goals. And, the more we engage our employees in cocreating the outcomes, the more we establish a virtuous circle of trust.

We certainly want to avoid having the employee feeling like their every action is being dictated. An employee is not a marionette. As Mihaly Czikszentmihalyi states:

> A worker who feels micromanaged soon loses interest in her job. The two most often cited complaints about jobs are lack of variety and conflicts with a supervisor. Both of these stem from a feeling that one has been reduced to a tool without choice or voice in the enterprise. Under such conditions workers will at most give only what is expected of them, but rarely more... A need for control from above must be balanced against the need for autonomy that even the humblest person holds dear.[1]

Another way managers overexert control is the way in which they manage people's time. The misguided focus on how many hours people work (as opposed to what they actually accomplish), so prevalent in the United States, is counter-productive. In his recent book *What Were They Thinking?*, Jeffrey Pfeffer points out the futility of this approach:

> It's time for the U.S. companies that have made late nights and short weekends a test of loyalty to come to terms with the myth that long hours and no vacations are good for the bottom line. In a business world ever more reliant on creative work and intellectual capital, taking care of the people whom you expect to be the source of your success seems like a better strategy.[2]

Pfeffer explains that, with time as a scarce commodity, organizations would be more likely to strive for efficient work practices and avoid unnecessary meetings. In addition, relaxed people are more likely to be refreshed, productive, and creative.[3] Again, there are circumstances in which certain coverage is needed, but even that issue can be minimized with multiple shifts and job-sharing. We shouldn't ignore the fact that working excessive hours reduces productivity. And we shouldn't let the fact that some workers need to work standard hours drive us to an arbitrary decision that everyone must work standard hours. Fortunately, organizations are getting wise to the need for flexibility, especially when it comes to knowledge workers. Mihaly Czikszentmihalyi notes:

> Few aspects of work have changed so much in the last decades as the rigidity of scheduling; the trend has become increasingly a return to a more flexible allocation of time. It is estimated that currently up to 40 percent of knowledge workers in the United States work nonstandard hours. At many companies, such as the Gallup Organization, in Nebraska, employees negotiate the time a task is expected to be accomplished, and then they are free to do it at night or the weekends while staying at home during the week.[4]

With such freedom, can people be truly accountable? Can we ensure productivity? Let's look at a few examples of organizations that have simultaneously achieved freedom, accountability, and, yes, productivity (not to mention the chaordic state we spoke of in Chapter 6).

Controlled Chaos

The Orpheus Chamber Orchestra, as discussed in Jeffrey Pfeffer's book *What Were They Thinking?*, is unique in that they have no conductor. Critically acclaimed, they have won a Grammy Award and consistently receive rave reviews from audiences worldwide. About the only "boss" they have is a managing director, who is more of a facilitator than a leader. Each member of the orchestra acts as a leader, with leadership functions shared and/or rotated among the members. Members construct the orchestra's musical programs, plan and conduct fundraising efforts, and take turns representing key positions, such as first violinist (assuming one is a violinist, of course). As Pfeffer notes, in most orchestras, everyone is centered on the conductor, who orchestrates their actions. Here, everyone is accountable.[5]

This works well in a small, volunteer-based organization, but can it work in a large organization? Or would the system fall prey to the opposite adage, "If everyone is accountable, nobody is accountable"?

If enough attention is spent on increasing employee satisfaction and removing systemic barriers to success, if people are working in their areas of strength, and if leaders provide guidance, principles, and desired outcomes, it is likely that such an approach can be successful. Without these caveats, such a system would turn to chaos in a large organization.

As reported recently in *Business Week*, electronics giant Best Buy has been experimenting with a concept called the Results-Only Work Environment (ROWE). The premise is that workers are focused on achieving evidence-based outcomes, regardless of the hours they work or where they work. Some examples of the 13 ROWE guideposts are:

#1: People at all levels stop doing any activity that is a waste of their time, the customer's time, or the company's money.

#7: Nobody talks about how many hours they work.

#9: It's O.K. to take a nap on Tuesday afternoon, grocery shop on Wednesday morning, or catch a movie on Thursday afternoon.[6]

The concept of ROWE was created by two human resources managers at Best Buy, Jody Thompson and Cali Ressler, who have since left the company to form CultureRx (www.culturerx.com), an organization dedicated to promoting the ROWE model. At Best Buy, the ROWE program began as a covert grassroots initiative. Thompson and Ressler began with one management group that was having serious problems with employee engagement. From there, it spread to other groups. Departments adopting the program showed dramatic improvements in employee retention and engagement (not to mention an average improvement in productivity of 35 percent). It wasn't until these statistics began coming in that Thompson and Ressler introduced the program to CEO Brad Anderson, who encourages bottom-up creativity. Now, based on documented successes, 75 percent of Best Buy's corporate workforce is in a Results-Only Work Environment, and engagement and productivity continue to shine.[7]

Some might question whether people can be trusted with so much freedom. In fact, when people are entrusted with achieving results, they feel more accountable than ever. As Best Buy's senior vice-president and general manager of the Dot Com division, John "J.T." Thompson reported, "For years I had been focused on the wrong currency. I was always looking to see if people were here. I should have been looking at what they were getting done."[8]

Although the ROWE model focuses on clear objectives, it adopts a different mindset from the traditional Management by Objectives (MBO) approach. In the MBO model, employees are given objectives that are SMART (Specific, Measurable, Agreed-to, Realistic, and Time-constrained), and the employees are evaluated on whether the objectives were achieved. An inherent problem with the MBO model is that success in reaching objectives is often dependent on a myriad of variables, including other people, external factors, and system effectiveness. In other words, the ability to achieve objectives is often beyond the control of the employee.

With the ROWE model, some of these limiting factors are offset by providing unprecedented freedoms, as evidenced by the preceding examples. Research has shown that, with this flexible approach, workers are more engaged and actively seek clear expectations. In addition, it is considered a normal part of the process to adjust expected outcomes when needed. As Thompson and Ressler stated, in a response to my inquiry about how exceptions are handled:

> In a Results-Only Work Environment, just like in a traditional work environment, delays can occur in a project. Some delays are obviously out of anyone's control. In these situations, employees inform their managers of the situation, and the goal components or timelines shift accordingly. We have recognized that in a traditional work environment, these delays are much more common than they are in a ROWE. Based on CultureRx's culture audit data, we have proof that ROWE work teams become more proactive and planful. They are constantly monitoring the landscape and know, very quickly, when something is going to cause a delay—they either course correct it very early on or successfully address the delay by resetting their timeline.[9]

The ROWE model appears to be an effective way to integrate freedom, accountability, and productivity. It lets people identify the best ways to achieve outcomes, allows them to suggest changes to outcomes, and encourages them to report systemic barriers to success. In this way, it combines an outcomes focus with a systems focus. To implement such change is an evolution, not a revolution. As it evolves, questions will arise regarding its impact on regulatory requirements, performance evaluations, and incentives, many of which are already beginning to be addressed by Best Buy and CultureRx. We will examine considerations for evaluations and incentives in more detail in Chapter 10. Meanwhile, it's hard to argue with the results.

Ricardo Semler, author of *Maverick* and *The Seven-Day Weekend*, and president of Semco, a Brazilian organization, has also achieved staggering results with a flexible work environment (among other unprecedented freedoms)—for more than two decades. At Semco, which has businesses as diversified as outsourcing management, environmental site remediation, engineering risk management, and others, employees make their own hours and have input to their own salaries. There are no job titles, permanent offices, or even an official organizational structure. Financials are published internally as part of an open-book system. As opposed to merely focusing on strategy and revenue as most companies do, Semco focuses on employee satisfaction and engagement. As a result, their revenue has been growing at a rate of 40 percent a year for two decades.[10] This is yet another example of a Virtuous Circle in which everyone benefits.

Although the details may vary, Best Buy and Semco seem to have found the right mix of vigilance and delegation. According to a recent *CIO Magazine* article, so have McGraw-Hill, Cisco, and Deloitte, organizations that have also implemented flexible work schedules with similar results.[11]

What's surprising is that organizations are more concerned about vigilance over their employees, and less concerned about vigilance over their leaders. If vigilance is needed, it is in ensuring our leaders create the right environment for success. Semco does this by asking employees to complete an anonymous survey about their managers. The survey asks questions about whether the manager listens to suggestions, shares credit, treats people fairly, and other such topics. The process has proven successful, transforming a number of autocratic managers into active listeners—not a small feat.[12] This is also a proven way to truly create an organizational culture. Value statements alone won't do it. All too often, an organization announces an enlightened culture, only to have autocratic managers in its midst setting the "real, unspoken" culture. The true culture ends up depending on which manager one works for. I call this "organizational schizophrenia." Having employees evaluate their managers, and taking those evaluations seriously, can ensure that the *stated* culture becomes the *real* culture. Even better would be to establish an open and ongoing dialogue with people at all levels of the organization.

Let's look at one more example in which freedom has produced surprisingly positive results. In late 2006, the European Union launched a program in seven cities, including Ejby in Denmark, Ipswich in England, Ostende in Belgium, and others, whereby all traffic signs and lights were removed. That meant no stop signs, no parking meters or restricted hours, no lines on streets, no crosswalk signs, and so on. In extremely hazardous areas, traffic lights were replaced by roundabouts. If this sounds like a recipe for pandemonium, you may be surprised to learn that the result was a dramatic decrease in traffic accidents. Drivers suddenly felt accountable and thought more about their actions, as did pedestrians. If drivers wanted to make a turn, they'd raise their arm out the window. People would nod politely to each other.[13]

Even the representatives from the United States and Britain who visited these areas were impressed. England is now testing this concept in their Kensington area.[14] It remains to be seen if this approach is scalable to larger cities, and whether culture plays a part in its success. For instance, do those countries that are more accustomed to rules have a harder or easier time with this approach, or are the results consistent regardless of culture? So far, the results appear consistent across cultures. For now, one thing is certain: freedom and accountability *can* coexist.

Blameless Reporting

It is hard to imagine an industry in which account-ability is more critical than in health care. In Chapter 3, we explored the phrase "To do no harm," which is a fundamen-tal principle among health care providers. In *To Do No Harm*, a book that outlines ways to ensure patient safety, authors Julianne Morath and Joanne Turnbull discuss lessons from High-Reliability Organizations, or HROs. HROs include those in aviation, nuclear power, military operations, space travel, and others in which reliability is necessarily high and accountability is critical. A key commonality among these organizations is a culture of blameless reporting. The authors outline a number of critical elements that have made HROs successful at adopting such an approach:

- Focusing on near-misses, not just reported accidents
- Providing incentives for voluntary reporting
- Guaranteeing confidentiality, as opposed to anonymity (the only exceptions being accidents and criminal activity, which are reported separately via mandatory reporting)
- Focusing on understanding, more than accounting
- Emphasizing a systemic view; examining multi-causal factors
- Allowing for narrative stories when reporting
- Ensuring reports are analyzed by an independent party in the organization

- Leading by example; directors should report as well
- Using the knowledge to continuously improve checklists and raise awareness[15]

Morath and Turnbull make particular reference to a children's hospital in Minnesota that recently implemented a Web-based reporting system. The online form asks five simple questions:

1. What happened?
2. Has it happened before?
3. Could it happen again?
4. What caused it to happen?
5. Who should be told?[16]

No doubt, a blameless reporting system combined with a culture of learning can go a long way toward building trust and accountability in any industry. As Morath and Turnbull put it:

Reciprocal accountability is based on trust. Managers trust that individuals [on the front lines] will call out errors, failures, risks, and hazards, and individuals [on the front lines] must trust that that the organization's management will listen and take action without retribution or blame.[17]

When trust is broken on either end, everybody loses. In a culture in which leaders act more as architects and maintainers of systems, and less as directors, their people can flourish and this breach of trust can be avoided.

Systems and People

In a collaborative and learning culture, systems are continuously improved based on lessons learned, assuming people feel free to share the lessons. As we discovered earlier, while people can certainly make mistakes, it is frequently the systems that are at fault and in need of correction. The more we correct systems, the less vigilant we must be in monitoring our people. Indeed, this creates a new leadership paradigm, as Pfeffer and Sutton suggest:

> Leaders often have the most positive impact when they help build systems where the actions of a few powerful and magnificently skilled people matter least. Perhaps the best way to view leadership is as the task of architecting organizational systems, teams, and cultures—as establishing the conditions and preconditions for others to succeed.[18]

In recognizing the importance of systems, we must not forget the human element. As we have seen, we can only correct systems if people feel engaged enough to contribute. They will not feel engaged if their unique strengths aren't being called upon or if they feel manipulated. One of the greatest barriers to this is the view of people as "resources." Managers frequently attempt to assemble a team of clones, in an effort to create "interchangeable parts." Sometimes they plan roles without regard for which individuals will be filling those roles. Often, they seek to create "foolproof" processes, so that even chimpanzees couldn't make a mistake, only to find that people don't follow the processes. Good systems take individual traits into account.

Acclaimed technology author and strategist Alistair Cockburn wrote a paper titled "Characterizing People as Non-Linear, First-Order Components in Software Development." He takes a decidedly people-centric view of systems:

> In the title, I refer to people as "components." That is how people are treated in the process/methodology design literature. The mistake in this approach is that "people" are highly variable and non-linear, with unique success and failure modes. Those factors are first-order, not negligible factors. Failure of process and methodology designers to account for them contributes to the sorts of unplanned project trajectories we so often see.[19]

Cockburn also suggests that people are predisposed to inconsistency; thus rigid methodologies often fail in practice. He argues that good, simple foundations in communication are more effective than rigid processes. He cautions that methodologies must consider how people vary, from day to day and group to group, and that universal approaches aren't appropriate. Finally, he points out that people generally like to make a difference.[20]

Leading teams to greatness, while at the same time celebrating people's individuality, is an art. In his landmark book *Organizing Genius*, leadership legend Warren Bennis discusses how to achieve what he calls "Great Groups":

Inevitably, the leader of a Great Group has to invent a leadership style that suits it. The standard models, especially the command-and-control style, simply won't work. The heads of Great Groups have to act decisively, but never arbitrarily. They have to make decisions without limiting the perceived autonomy of the other participants. Devising and maintaining an atmosphere in which others can put a dent in the universe is the leader's creative act.[21]

This view of a leader as a creative architect of systems and teams is a dramatic change from the traditional directive approach, but it can yield dividends!

Situational Leadership and Delegation

A helicopter, a porpoise, and a seagull make a helpful, if unusual, analogy for understanding the dynamics of leadership. Fons Trompenaars coined the term *helicopter view* to illustrate the ability of leaders to see both the forest and the trees. Trompenaars also refers to the *porpoise style* of leadership to describe the ability to remain near the surface, only to dive deep when needed.[22]

This is in contrast to the *seagull style* of leadership, which many people use to refer to those leaders who suddenly swoop down, make a lot of noise, make a mess over everything, and fly off. By building a helicopter view, we'll be in a better position to practice porpoise style leadership and avoid seagull style leadership.

Not only do we need to dive deep occasionally for certain types of problems, but we need to be more vigilant with certain individuals as well. To be arbitrarily vigilant is to micromanage. To be completely removed at all times is to be negligent. To obtain the right balance, we need to practice situational leadership.

The best-known situational leadership model was created by Paul Hersey and Ken Blanchard in the late 1960s. In the model, they define four styles of leadership, which should be matched to the development or readiness level of the employee. The leadership styles and corresponding development levels are as follows:

Leadership Styles		Employee Development Levels	
S1: Directing Leader	Assigns roles and tasks to the employee and monitors him or her closely	D1: Low Competence, High Commitment	Energetic and committed, but lacks the skills, knowledge, or ability required for the job
S2: Coaching Leader	Assigns roles and tasks, but encourages two-way communication and seeks input from the employee	D2: Some Competence, Low Commitment	Has some relevant skills, but needs guidance

Leadership Styles		Employee Development Levels	
S3: Support-ing Leader	Allows the employee to determine tasks and make day-to-day decisions, with input from the leader	D3: High Com-petence, Variable Commit-ment	Capable, but lacks confidence and/or motivation
S4: Delegating Leader	Allows the employee to operate independently and decide when the leader's input is needed	D4: High Compe-tence, High Commit-ment	Experienced and confident, and can operate at least as well as the leader

23

In the Hersey and Blanchard model, the leader must be able to adopt a leadership style appropriate to the situa-tion, as opposed to having one universal style. In fact, the leadership style could vary among different tasks for the same person, since an employee may be highly developed in one area but need more guidance in another.

Another model that is worth mentioning is "The Four Stages of Competence," also referred to as "The Learning Ladder." While this is not a situational leadership model *per se*, it is a useful tool for individuals to understand their competence level at certain tasks and to know when to seek help. Reports on this model's origins vary. Some sources date it as far back as Socrates or Confucius, but its modern form has been in psychology books since the

1980s. The four stages are as follows (I've paraphrased the explanations):

	Four Stages	Explanation
1.	Unconscious Incompetence	Everyone knows you're clueless except you. You don't realize why or when you're not achieving results and are surprised when people complain.
2.	Conscious Incompetence	The light bulb goes on. You suddenly "get it" and realize you need to do something different. You begin taking actions to change.
3.	Conscious Competence	You're becoming more confident and accomplishing goals through checklists, reading, learning, and mentoring. Things don't feel totally natural yet, nor should they, but you're achieving small successes.
4.	Unconscious Competence	This is the ultimate goal. Some call it situational awareness. The French call it *coup d'oeil*. It's like riding a bike or driving a car, and only happens with adequate experience and trial and error.

One might say that organizations, and not just individuals, go through these same stages.

When delegating work, a last model we should consider is Mihaly Csikszentmihalyi's "flow" model. Flow can be described as being "in the groove"—so engaged in your work you lose all concept of time. Think of a great skier or master musician. A key element of flow is that the work is rewarding in itself. The goal of achieving flow is to match a high level of challenge with a high level of skill in being able to meet the challenge. A simplified version of it is as follows:

Levels	Description
Low Skill, Low Challenge	Typically breeds apathy
Low Skill, High Challenge	Typically causes frustration and anxiety
High Skill, Low Challenge	Can bring contentment and build confidence, but the challenges must increase to encourage true engagement
High Skill, High Challenge	Desired focused state, where flow is achieved

24

As a side benefit to this, by offering increasing challenges appropriate to their skills, we can get people engaged who typically may show little or no initiative. Often, if people are not engaged, it is because they are not challenged with meaningful work. They don't have that feeling of "making a dent." If they did, we might not need as much vigilance. In essence, we can gain more control over outcomes by paying attention to people's readiness, and delegating and/or coaching accordingly, than by judging their performance.

The Impact of Technology on Delegation

Technology is advancing at rapid speeds and continues to force change upon us. It is already difficult to imagine an organization without the Internet and e-mail. Soon it will be hard to imagine an organization without blogs, wikis, social networks, and advanced mobile technology. Already, services such as Ning.com allow anyone to create a social network on the order of MySpace or Facebook, absolutely free. And, with the Intel-led effort to roll out WiMax (Worldwide Interoperability of Microwave Access), people will be wired to the Internet wherever they are, at lightning speeds, through cell phones, laptops, televisions, and so on.

The information-enabled workforce is no longer a dream. It is a reality to which today's leaders must adapt. It creates a new leadership paradigm that relies less on hierarchical structure and more on shared accountability and awareness. This has a profound impact on the way we communicate and delegate work.

In Chapter 5, we examined the importance of context, referencing a United States government-sponsored research report titled *Command Concepts*, from authors Builder, Bankes, and Nordin. According to the report, the U.S. Army has also been examining the changing dynamics of leadership, as evident in this excerpt from a U.S. Army developmental concept paper:

> *Future technology will require the Army to reassess the time-honored means of battle command—to recognize that in the future, military operations will involve the coexistence of both hierarchical and non-hierarchical processes. Order will be less physically-imposed than knowledge-imposed... Such shared information, where, in some cases, subordinates have as much knowledge as commanders, changes the dynamics of leadership in ways yet to be fully explored and exploited.*[25]

It takes a different kind of leader to take full advantage of these technological advances. It takes a leader who can embrace shared accountability. It takes a leader who knows when to lead and when to get out of the way. And it takes a leader who can understand the dynamics of virtual and mobile teams, which are becoming increasingly common.

For a hint at what an information-enabled organization could look like, we can look to nature. Ken Thompson, founder of Bioteams.com, studies the behavioral traits of bees, ants, geese, dolphins, and other species in order to glean lessons for business leaders. Thompson is a pioneer in this rapidly growing field. From a high level, his research has shown that nature's most effective teams share three common principles:

1. One-way communication is fine. Members of biological teams broadcast messages announcing an update, a need, or an opportunity. A response is not required or expected.

2. Everyone must broadcast. Shared accountability is expected. To enable such accountability, concise information must be readily available to everyone, and everyone must have a bias toward action.

3. Act, don't ask. Permission is granted. Nature's teams do not seek permission before acting.[26]

Human teams, of course, require some modifications to these rules. For instance, as Thompson notes, permission structures must be established that define when permission is truly required.[27] Aside from that, excessive approval requirements lead to delay, frustration, and eventually, apathy. Instead, we need to provide information, the technology to quickly share the information in all directions, and an environment in which people feel engaged and accountable.

Key Concepts

- To increase employees' self-esteem and ability to self-direct, we need to develop a positive connection with them, let them achieve actions and learn from mistakes, and provide specific outcomes that are in line with organizational goals.

- The misguided focus on how many hours people work is counter-productive. Organizations have been shown to achieve dramatic improvements in employee engagement and productivity by allowing greater work flexibility.

- Having employees evaluate their managers, and taking those evaluations seriously, is a proven way to ensure that the *stated* organizational culture becomes the *real* organizational culture.

- High-Reliability Organizations (HROs), including those in aviation, nuclear power, military operations, space travel, and others, have achieved greater shared accountability through a learning culture and blameless reporting.

- Systems are more frequently at fault for errors than are individuals. But, in recognizing the importance of systems, we must not forget the human element. Systems must be adaptable to various work habits and cultures.

- The view of a leader as a creative architect of systems and teams is a dramatic change from the traditional directive approach, but it can yield dividends.

- To be arbitrarily vigilant is to micromanage. To be completely removed is to be negligent. To obtain the right balance, we need to practice situational leadership.

- There are three models that should be considered when delegating: Hersey and Blanchard's situational leadership model, the "Four Stages of Competence" learning ladder, and Mihaly Csikszentmihalyi's "flow" model.

- Technology, such as blogs, wikis, social networks, and mobile devices, enables broader information sharing, distributed accountability, and less hierarchy. This has a profound impact on leadership and delegation.

? Questions to Ponder

1. In what ways do I tend to "do for" and "tell how"? How can I instead give people increasing challenges within their skill set?

2. Are mistakes punished in my organization? What impact might this have on people's desire to report needed system corrections? What actions can I take today to institute a blameless reporting system?

3. Do I practice situational leadership when delegating work, or do I adopt one leadership style and use it exclusively?

4. In what ways might I begin to use some of the models presented in this chapter, such as Hersey and Blanchard's situational leadership model, the "Four Stages of Competence" model, and Csikszentmihalyi's "flow" model?

5. Does the technology in my organization support effective communication and shared accountability? What changes can I make to better leverage technology?

Notes

Get even more from this book. Visit **www.rmcpublications.com/grayareas** to share your thoughts and questions on topics in this chapter and to access additional resources.

Chapter 8
Appearance vs. Substance

"The world more often rewards the appearance of merit than merit itself."

- François de la Rochefoucauld

Fundamental Question:

Which should I address first—appearance or substance? Where can I most afford to make sacrifices, and when?

Is it more important to focus on creating the perception of an appealing and responsive organization, or is it best to first ensure efficient work processes? Given a limited budget, should an organization first address that which is apparent to the customer/public, or the back-end efficiencies within the organization? Should development of new products be focused on aesthetic design or practical usefulness?

All of these questions require us to evaluate both appearance and substance and to make tradeoffs where necessary. Let's examine the nature of each and discover how finding the right balance impacts how we address our relationships—and how we design our products.

The Importance of Appearance

To the public, perception is reality. This is why organizations spend fortunes on advertising, marketing, and public relations. Organizations rightfully want to project a positive image and increase the perceived value of their products and services.

In the sixteenth century, Niccolò Machiavelli encouraged rulers under his tutelage to patronize the arts, support trade guilds, and hold elaborate events, all for the purpose of keeping up appearances. He even suggested appearing liberal, although he didn't necessarily support *being* liberal. As he stated, "For the great majority of mankind are satisfied with appearance, as though they were realities and are often more influenced by the things that seem than by those that are."

More recently, in an article in *USA Today* on the public's fascination with appearance, philosophy professor Gerald F. Kreyche noted:

Although people loudly proclaim that "appearances are deceptive," they still tend to accept appearance over reality. Despite the adage that "one can't tell a book by its cover" or a record by its cover jacket, both often are sold on that very basis.[1]

Knowing how important appearance is, one would be foolish not to give it serious attention. For a leader, appearance can cause great things to happen. Indeed, a leader who appears confident can inspire people and make them feel secure. As Pfeffer and Sutton point out:

Everyone expects leaders to matter a lot...Leaders need to act as if they are in control, project confidence, and talk about the future, even while recognizing and acknowledging the organizational realities and their own limitations.[2]

Without a doubt, the perception of our audience is something that every leader should be concerned about.

Appearance as a Self-Fulfilling Prophecy

An important side benefit to focusing on appearance is that the image we bestow upon others—or ourselves—can be a self-fulfilling prophecy.

Between 1924 and 1932, Harvard University professors Elton Mayo, Fritz Roethlisberger, and William J. Dixon conducted a series of experiments at a Western Electric factory called the Hawthorne Works. The original purpose of the experiments was to determine the effect of lighting on workers' productivity. After discovering that productivity increased regardless of whether the illumination changed, the researchers began to realize that just the fact of being observed changed the way people acted. They felt important because they were being observed, and thus their productivity increased (at least temporarily). This premise came to be known as the *Hawthorne effect*.

Realizing that people worked harder when they felt more important, the professors began experimenting with more overt powers of suggestion. When workers were actively engaged in the experiments and treated on par with the research scientists, they began making surprising contributions, in many cases surpassing all expectations of their capabilities.

The lesson from this is that people will live up to—or down to—the image we bestow upon them. As leaders, we must be aware of the ripple effect this can create. If we attach a certain image to someone, we will treat him or her accordingly, others with whom we share this image will treat him or her accordingly, and ultimately, he or she will act accordingly.

Appearances do more than just create a perception; they actually can influence who people become. Thus, appearance becomes substance.

Appearance as Substance: A Design Perspective

The relationship between appearance and substance is also relevant when designing our products. Consider the two primary elements of design—form and function. Should development of new products be focused on aesthetic appeal (form) or practical usefulness (function)?

The maxim "Form follows function" is a principle popularized by famed American architect Louis Sullivan in 1896. (His original statement was "Form ever follows function.") Sullivan favored a minimalist approach, only including what would contribute to function. His assistant, Frank Lloyd Wright, endorsed this approach as well. Most modern architects assert that Sullivan was not saying form is not important, merely that it should have a certain function in mind. The premise is that pure ornament should be avoided.

Yet there is something to be said for ornament. If something serves to provide aesthetic appeal or some sort of symbolic meaning, isn't that in itself a function, albeit one that cannot be quantified? This is why we have various types and colors of fabric, wood trim on luxury automobile interiors, and corporate branding. In an article titled "Beyond Budget" in *PM Network* magazine, Carlyle Maranhao, a client principal with Hewlett-Packard, uses the example of building a bridge. He states, "... if it was built on time, on budget, and met specs, but wasn't beautiful to look at, it may not have enhanced the city it was in." In cases where beauty or ornament serves a purpose, appearance is substance. Form *is* function.[3]

Information presentation guru Edward Tufte often lectures on effective Web site design. He notes that the top ten most frequently visited Web sites have more than 100 links on their front pages. He also suggests that Web pages should reserve at least 80 percent of the space for content, including pertinent links, relevant data, and content-rich diagrams. When designing Web pages, as in many forms of media, content is king. Yet Tufte also advises that certain colors, such as earthy tones, are more relaxing to people. Again, aesthetic appearance serves a valuable, although nonquantitative, function. As Albert Einstein said, "Not everything that can be counted counts, and not everything that counts can be counted."

Organizations are beginning to see the power in good aesthetic design. In fact, one might say that a design revolution is underway. Organizations such as Apple, LG, and Samsung have leaped ahead of the pack based on their attention to design. IBM, Hewlett-Packard, and Johnson & Johnson have all recently appointed vice presidents for design. According to a recent study, many companies are now looking for design majors instead of MBAs when recruiting their executives.

If content is king, then, certainly, design is queen.

When Appearances Deceive

While attention to appearance is important, we want to avoid creating a *Potemkin Village*, named for Grigori Potemkin, who in 1787 allegedly built an elaborate façade of a village in Ukraine to fool the visiting Catherine the Great. The story may be a myth, but the name stuck and is used today to indicate a superficial appearance with a hollow substance. Let's look at a few examples.

Politicians and business leaders sometimes hire spin-doctors to put an intentionally misleading slant on events, hoping to shape or change public opinion. Typically this is done through omitting certain points, citing unproven truths, communicating bad news when it is least likely to be noticed, or issuing intentionally vague or generic statements. Frequently, the public becomes wise to the ruse.

In ancient Rome, Julius Caesar gave the appearance of working with a senate (which was, in fact, stacked with his supporters). People ultimately grew wise to the fact that he was a dictator overstepping his boundaries. Eventually, he was murdered by his own people on the Ides of March in 44 B.C.

Mark Hurst runs a great blog site on customer experience, called Good Experience. He posted an interesting entry about his experience ordering a file cabinet from an office supply store. The ordering process was easy enough. After the cabinet was delivered, however, he discovered the overall construction was flimsy and the top drawer didn't close right. He called the company and immediately got a human being on the phone (something rare these days). The person was very friendly and polite, but proceeded to inform him that the company didn't offer refunds, only exchanges.[4]

As Hurst notes, the customer service was excellent, but the customer experience was far from it.[5] From all appearances, the company looked professional and put on a good face to the customer. Behind a nice façade, however, the product quality was poor, as were the company's policies. They lacked substance.

Many organizations run into this scenario when investing in software systems. With a limited budget, they struggle with choices such as deciding between investing in their back-office systems or in a Customer Relationship

Management (CRM) system that will help them better meet customer needs. There is no definitive answer to this dilemma, but a few guidelines on ensuring adequate substance can serve us well. Safety and regulatory requirements must come first. Severe quality problems that will impact customer satisfaction must come second.

Mark Kozak-Holland has written several books on lessons from the Titanic disaster, and he often speaks on the topic. Two examples he likes to point out clearly illustrate the dangers of focusing only on superficial appearances. In the first example, Bruce Ismay, the director of the Titanic, insisted on fewer lifeboats in order to avoid blocking the ocean views of the rich passengers in the first class suites. Second, Ismay insisted on building a grandiose 200-foot ballroom, despite the fact that it meant compromising the ship's bulkhead. In both of these cases, the architects were aware of the dangers, but they succumbed to executive pressure. Many people died as a result of these two deficiencies.

A customer can accept minor flaws. Thus, it is not necessary to wait for perfection. If fundamental safety and/or regulatory needs are addressed and minor flaws don't impact basic usability, we can then concentrate on good customer relations. As we learned from Marcus Buckingham and Curt Coffman in Chapter 6, a customer's primary need is accuracy, then availability. Only after satisfying those needs are we ready to progress to delivering partnership and advice.

As we've seen from these examples, to focus on a good image without ensuring at least adequate back-end quality is to create the appearance of customer care without the substance behind it. The best customer relations in the world cannot make up for unsafe or unusable products or inaccurate services. Inadequate attention to substance will quickly reveal false appearances.

When Tradeoffs Are Needed

Generally, marketing, sales, and creative specialists are focused on appearance, while engineers are focused on functionality. Sometimes, however, tradeoffs must be made. This is where collaboration and creativity come in. For example, Fons Trompenaars often tells of how Bang and Olufsen (B&O), the elite audio/visual electronics company, refused for years to make sacrifices in either aesthetic design or functionality. This hurt them financially. Then, CEO Anders Knutsen came along and added a much-needed touch of creativity and cooperation. As Trompenaars notes:

> B&O has never made concessions to either side, and, therefore, manufactured unaffordable products. By the introduction of Idealand, in which engineers, designers, production people, and marketers cooperate, Knutsen has managed to create a synthesis that has saved B&O from financial ruin... This synthesis of harmonious products that has been achieved in Idealand has been the result of stimulating dialogue between diverse groups of professionals.[6]

Indeed, creativity and collaboration are vital in achieving the healthy integration of design and functionality— appearance and substance.

Key Concepts

- To the public, perception is reality.

- A leader who appears confident can inspire people and make them feel secure.

- Appearance can influence who we become. People live up—or down—to the image we bestow upon them.

- There is inherent danger in creating the perception of an appealing and responsive organization without at least an adequate system to support it.

- If something serves to provide aesthetic appeal or some sort of symbolic meaning, it is providing a valuable function, albeit one that cannot be quantified.

- Creativity and collaboration of diverse groups are vital in making necessary tradeoffs in design versus function.

? Questions to Ponder

1. In what ways can I boost the image of people on my staff and encourage them to live up to that image?

2. Do I give equal attention to outward appearances of my products and services (i.e., the marketing perspective) and the quality of those products and services?

3. When developing products or services, do I give attention to the value that aesthetic appearance or symbolic meaning may bring?

4. When making tradeoffs in design versus function, do I engage diverse groups, such as engineering and marketing, to integrate alternate perspectives?

Notes

Get even more from this book. Visit **www.rmcpublications.com/grayareas** to share your thoughts and questions on topics in this chapter and to access additional resources.

Chapter 9
Centralization vs. Decentralization

"It is amazing what you can accomplish if you do not care who gets the credit."

- Harry S. Truman

Fundamental Question:

Which work should be done centrally and which distributed? Where should decision making lie?

Anyone in business for more than five years has seen the pendulum swing from centralization to decentralization and back again more than once. Some organizations hype the control and economies of scale gained from centralizing, and others tout the flexibility they achieve from decentralizing.

There is no doubt that we can gain efficiencies and economic advantages by centralizing certain business functions, at least in the short term. For instance, we can avoid redundancies by providing customer service from a central office instead of having service reps at each location. We can purchase materials and products in bulk at significant savings. And we can gain a stronger position when negotiating contracts centrally.

There is some debate over whether these advantages are worthwhile in the long term. For instance, will centralized service reps be able to build customer relationships the way local reps can (especially the local reps that have been in their positions for years)? Will a single vendor be able to meet the specialized demands of local or regional branches and retain close relationships with those branches? These concerns are enough to dissuade some organizations from centralizing their customer service and procurement functions. Take Semco, for example. Ricardo Semler describes the benefits of what he calls "manufacturing cells," in which decentralized groups of workers manage their own areas independently:

Can I definitely say our manufacturing cells have made Semco more profitable? Some of the plusses and minuses have been tricky to tally. True, our manufacturing cells don't respect the so-called economies of scale. Instead of buying, say, twenty machine casings at a time, we tend to buy casings in much smaller quantities, since many items are stocked right in the cell and there's no space for extras. That is more expensive than buying in bulk.

Then again, maintaining large inventories of casings can tie up capital. Our inventory levels have fallen to ridiculously low levels, and each year we do away with more and more stocking space... And the cells have made people work much more closely, so our plants are much more finely tuned. This can be translated into more productivity.[1]

Regarding overall leadership, again there is debate as to what and how much should be centralized. Philosopher Jean-Jacques Rousseau once said, "It is unnatural for a majority to rule, for a majority can seldom be organized and united for specific action, and a minority can." To a degree, this is true. A centralized minority (i.e., management) can come to agreement quickly and exert more control. However, this assumes that the minority understands enough to make correct decisions and set correct policies.

Often, that is not the case. Consider the comments of British politician Joshua Toulmin Smith:

> *Centralization is that system of government under which the smallest number of minds, and those knowing the least, and having the fewest opportunities of knowing it... and having the smallest interest in the well working, have the management of it, or the control over it.*

Having a central body that frequently makes uninformed decisions also serves to lower morale for those who are out in the field and must live with the consequences.

While it is hard to ignore these concerns about centralization, we also need to ensure consistency and efficiency in our organizations. Is there a proper balance between centralization and decentralization? Is there a definitive model we can follow?

Unfortunately, there is not. There are, however, good examples of those who have found a way to achieve the advantages of a large organization without sacrificing flexibility and local feel. But first, they had to understand the power of decentralization.

Starfish, Geese, and Sea Monsters

Ori Brafman and Rod Beckstrom wrote a wonderful and thought-provoking book called *The Starfish and the Spider.* The title takes its name from the fact that a spider will die if its head is cut off, but if you cut off a starfish's leg, it will grow a new leg, and the leg that was cut off can spawn an entirely new starfish. That's because the major organs are replicated throughout each leg. The authors compare the traditional, hierarchical organization to the spider. A new breed of organization is emerging that more closely resembles the starfish.[2]

Early in their book, Brafman and Beckstrom tell the story about Dave Garrison, a newly hired CEO of Netcom, one of the first Internet service providers. During a financial crunch, Garrison tried to raise funds from French bankers, but they refused to help him. The bankers could not accept that there was no president of the Internet. Before they would shell out money, they needed to know that there was a president who would provide the structure so that the Internet would remain a significant force.[3]

The authors go on to tell of how Alcoholics Anonymous grew out of a common set of ideals with just a few simple rules. They also highlight organizations such as eMule, a popular file sharing network that has no clear leader. The authors even go so far as to reference al Qaeda as an example of a decentralized organization. They note that, after September 11, 2001, the United States' search for the head of al Qaeda was not unlike the French bankers trying to identify the president of the Internet.[4]

What Brafman and Beckstrom have identified is no less than the connective tissue that holds a decentralized organization together. This connective tissue is made up of two elements: *information* and *shared ideals.* Effective decentralized organizations share these two ingredients. In that sense, they are not unlike a typical franchise, except that a franchise has an identifiable hierarchy and a more clearly mandated infrastructure. As the authors note, if property or money are involved at an organizational level, the organization by default must have *some* form of central body. The question is which functions should be centralized and to what extent.

Before we explore organizational structures, let's see what other lessons nature has to offer us about the advantages of decentralization. In Chapter 7, we learned about Ken Thompson's research on biological teams. In addition to his studies of ants, bees, and dolphins, he also studies geese. As Thompson discovered, when geese fly in formation and suddenly change direction, it's not based on some sudden insight from the leader. It's based on the fact that the leader no longer knows where to go, and another goose needs to take over at the helm of the flock.[5] The geese do this instinctively. They act as *emergent leaders.* There is evidence to show that some of the best leadership comes from those who emerge to help fulfill a mission, and not those who are simply assigned the leadership role. Through observation, we can see who these emergent leaders are. The answers can sometimes surprise us. However, if everything is dictated from above, these emergent leaders will not have the opportunity or the incentive to reveal themselves.

M. Mitchell Waldrop wrote a book titled *Complexity: The Emerging Science at the Edge of Order and Chaos.* The book outlines his groundbreaking work with a number of physicists, mathematicians, and computer scientists (including some Nobel Laureates), as part of the Santa Fe Institute, a think tank for researching chaos, order, and interconnectedness. Craig Reynolds, a presenter at one of their workshops, demonstrated computer simulations of flocking behavior in birds. His computerized virtual versions were called "boids." He placed the boids into an online environment with various virtual obstacles. He programmed them with three simple guidelines:

1. Try to maintain a minimum distance from other objects (including other boids).
2. Try to match the velocity of nearby boids.
3. Try to move toward the perceived center of mass of nearby boids.[6]

As noted in the book, none of these rules directly said to form a flock. They merely gave each boid individual principles to follow. Yet in each simulation, the boids formed a flock, flying around obstacles and staying with the other boids in formation. In one case, a boid hit an obstacle and sped up to rejoin the group. It was not specifically programmed to act that way, aside from the three guidelines.[7]

As Chris Langton, another Santa Fe Institute participant, pointed out, "The most surprising lesson we have learned from simulating complex physical systems is that complex behavior need not have complex roots." He went on to add:

> Try doing that with a single set of top-level rules... The system would be impossibly cumbersome and complicated, with the rules telling each boid what to do in every conceivable situation... And besides, since it's effectively impossible to cover every conceivable situation, top-down systems are forever running into combinations of events they don't know how to handle.[8]

Langton goes on to describe how we can use these lessons in structuring our organizations:

> The way to achieve lifelike behavior is to simulate populations of simple units instead of one big complex unit. Use local control instead of global control. Let the behavior emerge from the bottom up, instead of being specified from the top down. And while you're at it, focus on ongoing behavior instead of the final result.[9]

We should also note that the three rules the boids were given were all about relationships. In her landmark book *Leadership and the New Science*, Meg Wheatley noted, "None of us exists independent of our relationships with others." This is the way nature works as well. As Wheatley points out, while Newtonian physics focuses on identifying the predictability of all things, quantum physics comes to terms with randomness. For instance, quantum physicists have discovered that particles take multiple forms depending on their relationships with other particles. Since many of these relationships are invisible, they are impossible to predict. Scientists have also observed that elementary particles, once paired, will still react to one another, even when separated by a great distance.[10]

To this day, scientists have not discovered why or how.

The lesson to us as leaders is this: *Relationships are dynamic, sometimes invisible, and extremely relevant, whether we are referring to particles or people.* More than exerting control or gaining predictability (which is usually a fruitless endeavor, anyway), we need to focus on managing relationships. In this way, we can truly be scalable as our organization grows. If information and shared ideals are the connective tissue of an organization, then relationships are the blood.

The giant siphonophore is a jellyfish-like sea creature of approximately 130 feet in length, which is larger than a blue whale. What makes this creature unique is that it is made up of a collection of specialized working parts, all of which work together as one being. None of the parts can live on their own, yet they all operate as independent entities, each with a specialized role (some catch prey, others digest food, others can swim, and so on). If the siphonophore bumps into an object, the whole creature, including all of its parts, illuminates. Somehow, it stays integrated and acts as one being.

With the siphonophore and other life forms, such as multicellular organisms (like us), nature has found a way to create a decentralized, yet integrated, entity. It does this through a combination of information, shared ideals, and relationships. There is no reason our organizations cannot do the same.

The Virtual Integrated Organization

For years, the United States Veterans Health Administration (VHA) stood out above all other health care institutions as a measure of poor quality and excessive bureaucracy. In fact, politicians often used this to make a case against socialized medicine.[11] Today, the picture is much different. (As a side note, the VHA is not to be confused with the Walter Reed Army Medical Center, which has recently come under fire amid reports of squalor and neglect. The Walter Reed facility is part of the U.S. military hospital system, which is a completely separate network.)

Consider the following facts regarding the VHA today:

- A *New England Journal of Medicine* study in 2003 found that veterans' health facilities ranked "significantly better" than fee-for-service Medicare facilities in all eleven quality measures analyzed.

- A recent *Annals of Internal Medicine* study reported that veterans' hospitals outshone commercial managed-care systems in all seven measures of diabetes treatment quality.

- The VHA recently won the prestigious seal of approval from The National Committee for Quality Assurance, outperforming the highest non-VHA hospitals in all seventeen performance measures.

- In a recent independent survey, 81 percent of VHA patients said they were satisfied with the care they received, as compared with 77 percent of Medicare and Medicaid patients.[12]

The VHA's turnaround began in 1994 when Ken Kizer, a former emergency-room physician, was named the VHA's Undersecretary of Health. When Kizer took on the challenge of revamping the VHA's horrific state of affairs, nobody suspected that they would go from "last to first."

The makeover was nothing less than a miracle. Kizer did this by transforming the organization from a collection of hospitals, managed centrally by Washington bureaucrats, to a regionally coordinated patient-focused network. His battle cry was "Health care, not hospitals."[13]

Kizer established a virtual, but integrated, organization through a network of hubs, which he called Veterans Integrated Service Networks (or VISNs). The idea was that each VISN would be a network of affiliated organizations for the purpose of providing full health care services to patients. Decisions would be made mostly at the VISN level, rather than coming from headquarters in Washington. The VISNs would be community-focused, providing local presence, yet with standardized quality based on leveraging national best practices. Unnecessary bureaucracy would be eliminated. For instance, no longer would approvals be required for small purchases.

In Kizer's model, the VISNs handle logistics and budgeting for their respective areas. They conduct demographic-based planning, align local resources, and provide an integrated array of care for patients of their collective facilities. In addition, the VISN leaders, along with internal and external stakeholders, form a council that makes recommendations to the VISN directors. This is a "whole product" approach, in that it leverages partnerships, alliances, and consortia when developing or marketing products or services.

With so much power distributed among the VISNs, one might ask: What's the role of headquarters? In the VHA system, Washington headquarters is responsible for providing guiding principles, change leadership, consulting, advice, and information services. In essence, the role of headquarters is to foster new behaviors and attitudes that further the goals of the overall organization.

To facilitate all of this, Kizer instituted sweeping changes to provide better visibility of information, make improvements in technology and training, and enable decentralized decision making.

Because of the changes Kizer influenced, every nurse and doctor in the network has instant access to electronic patient records, and prescriptions are filled robotically, avoiding mistakes common to most other hospitals. And because the VHA hospitals treat their patients for life, they spend more time and money on preventive care, as they realize it costs everyone less in the long run.

Unfortunately, Kizer made some enemies along the way. Several facilities needed to be shut down or moved, either because of demographics or because the buildings were too remote or badly neglected. Certain legislators took offense at this and barred the way to Kizer's reappointment. In 1999, he decided he'd had enough and walked away. "One thing I would do differently," he said, in a recent interview, "...would be spending more time with members of Congress on a personal level and holding the hands of some people in the veterans service organizations."[14]

As Kizer learned, relationships are vital.

An epilogue to this story is that, although Kizer's reforms lasted beyond his reign, Washington headquarters has been slowly adding bureaucracy back into the picture. Time will tell how far this will revert back and if this will impact the VHA's success rates.

The VHA isn't the only organization that has achieved great results through a decentralized, integrated network. Fons Trompenaars offers a variety of examples of organizations that have successfully integrated centralization with decentralization. For example, he tells how Heineken once ran an international TV advertisement campaign that was completely misinterpreted in one particular country because of a cultural difference. Heineken's response was to decentralize the campaign throughout Europe, allowing local countries to develop their own campaigns, in alignment with a core central theme (the campaigns had to portray Heineken as helping to transition someone from a stressed to a relaxed state). In the Caribbean, Heinken adopted a different theme (portraying Heineken with a metropolitan flair), but allowing variations within that theme for each island.[15] By having separate themes in Europe and the Caribbean, each with their own local variations, Heineken adopted what we might call a "multiple hub and spoke" model, much like the VHA did. Also like the VHA, overall guidance and support came from the central body.

According to Trompenaars and his partner, Charles Hampden-Turner, the relationship between centralization and decentralization should not be a matter of "either/or" or even "and/and," but instead should be viewed as a "through-through" relationship. The centralized body accumulates knowledge *through* the input of local experts and disseminates that knowledge throughout the organization. In turn, the local bodies improve their activity *through* leveraging the global body of knowledge. In other words, the centralized body is focused on the improvement of knowledge, while the local bodies are focused on the improvement of activity.[16] Each benefits *through* the other. Moreover, an organization can determine which rules and principles apply globally and can institute standards accordingly.

Rather than debate over global versus local, or centralization versus decentralization, we should instead be looking for ways to integrate both sides of the equation.

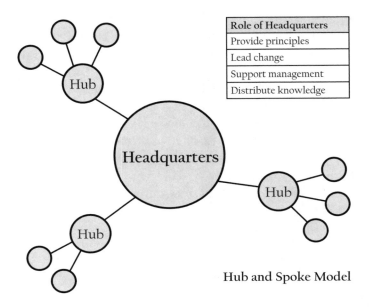

Role of Headquarters
Provide principles
Lead change
Support management
Distribute knowledge

Hub and Spoke Model

Fragmentation: A Word of Caution

In arranging what gets done locally versus globally, we must not overlook the customer experience.

Over the years, I've accumulated a list of bad customer experiences that I've personally encountered. In many cases, the cause was fragmentation. For example, a major bank in which I hold my accounts has separate divisions that handle telephone banking, Internet banking, and other services. I once called to change a recurring automatic payment and was subsequently directed to several departments to see which one initially set up my recurring payment. None of the parties had access to the whole picture of my account history.

In another case, the payroll company I use has a special department that addresses tax inquiries. This department is not directly accessible to the customer, except by fax. Making matters more difficult, the customer service representatives do not have access to the latest status of the tax inquiries, which makes them unable to properly address follow-up questions.

I once ordered an extra power cord for my laptop. When I called the computer company's customer service department to find why the part was more than a month late in being delivered, I was told that they didn't have access to the parts orders, only orders for new computers. I had to dial a different phone number to contact the parts department.

When setting up a new automobile lease for automatic payment, my first payment never went through. The finance company had the wrong account number due to a clerical error. They were unable to correct the information by phone because the account had been automatically frozen. I had to mail the payment with a form to a different department, so the account could be unlocked. Instead of making it easier for me to pay, they made it harder.

While these may seem like minor inconveniences, it's the little things that customers remember. Small interactions have big impacts. What all of these examples have in common is a lack of the connective tissue that decentralized organizations run on: information and shared ideals. They also reflect a lack of attention to the lifeblood of a decentralized organization—relationships (in these cases, the relationships with the customer and the relationships among departments). Instead, these organizations, like many others, focus internally, on each department's respective duties.

As the VHA and Heineken have learned, a decentralized, but integrated, organization whose employees are information-enabled, infused with the right ideals, and attentive to customers and partners, is a powerful model indeed.

Key Concepts

- There are economies of scale to be gained from centralizing certain business functions (such as purchasing and customer service), but there is debate over whether these advantages are worthwhile in the long term.

- A centralized minority can come to agreement quickly and exert more control. This assumes that the minority understands enough to make correct decisions and set correct policies. Often, that is not the case.

- The connective tissue of decentralized, but integrated, organizations consists of two main ingredients: information and shared ideals.

- Relationships are the lifeblood of any organization, especially decentralized organizations. Relationships are dynamic, sometimes invisible, and extremely relevant.

- Some of the best leadership comes from those who emerge to meet a challenge in difficult times. Through observation, we can see who these emergent leaders are. If everything is dictated from above, however, these emergent leaders will not reveal themselves.

- A "multiple hub and spoke" model, such as that employed by the VHA in its networked organization, and by Heineken in its marketing program, is an effective way to integrate local expertise with a global message.

- Experiments have shown that complex behavior does not necessarily have complex roots. Simple guidelines often work best.

- Decentralized organizations can benefit from having formal mechanisms by which to share information and best practices throughout the organization.
- A negative side effect of some decentralization efforts is fragmented customer service. This can be avoided with adequate attention to information, shared ideals, and relationships (both with customers and partners).

? Questions to Ponder

1. Does my organization extend decision-making authority to those closest to the action, or does it isolate decision making to a few select individuals? How can I better leverage the collective intelligence of my organization or team?

2. If I centralize certain functions, which relationships will be lost as a result? How will that impact my organization and its customers?

3. Are there mechanisms in place in my organization to facilitate the sharing of best practices?

4. Do I enable local or regional variations of my core messages, or do I assume one size fits all?

5. Are the people in my organization integrated through accessible information, shared ideals, and general guidelines?

6. Are the people in my organization required to follow complex rules and/or processes that inhibit their ability to innovate?

7. What internal and external relationships are necessary in order to serve my customers? How can I improve those relationships for the benefit of the customer?

8. Are there ways in which my organization or team is inadvertently providing a fragmented customer experience?

 Notes

Get even more from this book. Visit **www.rmcpublications.com/grayareas** to share your thoughts and questions on topics in this chapter and to access additional resources.

Section III
Tools for Managing the Gray Areas

Chapter 10
The Four Themes of Gray Area Management

*"True genius resides in the capacity for evaluation of
uncertain, hazardous, and conflicting information."*

                                    - Winston Churchill

When undertaking a journey, especially one through
the gray areas, the image we begin with isn't necessarily
the image we come away with. For example, when we began our journey through the seven gray areas identified and
discussed in this book, we approached them as opposing
dilemmas:

- Individual Needs *versus* Organizational Goals
- Generalists *versus* Specialists
- Big Picture *versus* Narrow Focus
- Structure *versus* Flexibility
- Vigilance *versus* Delegation
- Appearance *versus* Substance
- Centralization *versus* Decentralization

In each of these cases, we discovered that it's not a
matter of choosing one versus the other, but in finding the
right blend of the two. We've seen a variety of examples
and guidelines, and even those are not universal solutions.
Ultimately, every leader must make difficult choices that
they can live with. Often these choices are not between
right and wrong, but between right and right.[1]

Throughout our expedition, four common themes have emerged, interweaving their way through these seven gray areas. These themes can help us on our path to making better choices and, ultimately, to becoming better leaders. We can rely on them as we would rely on a compass when we're lost.

The four common themes of gray area management are as follows:

1. Ideals: Standing for Something
2. Leading by Questioning
3. Systems Thinking
4. Empathy and Cultural Awareness

Let's reexamine these themes with a finer lens to see how they can guide us in our everyday challenges.

Ideals: Standing for Something

Former U.S. Senate Chaplain Peter Marshall once said, "Give us clear vision, that we may know where to stand and what to stand for—because unless we stand for something, we shall fall for anything." Knowing what we stand for can provide much needed clarity when making decisions, guiding our priorities in the face of daily stress. Under pressure to meet economic needs and short-term results, it's all too easy to overlook our responsibility to multiple parties, including customers, employees, communities, and the world at large. In the midst of life's daily challenges, we sometimes forget that our actions and beliefs have far-reaching consequences. As Voltaire put it, "No snowflake in an avalanche ever feels responsible."

Some organizations seem to know what they stand for and choose to make a difference in the world. Toyota is legendary for its community- and people-focused principles, which it proves every day by its actions. Consider their number one principle, as stated in their "14 Principles of the Toyota Way," a doctrine that outlines their management beliefs: "Base your management decisions on a long-term philosophy, even at the expense of short-term financial goals." Another Toyota principle states, "Respect your extended network of partners and suppliers by challenging them and helping them improve."[2] With key measures that support these principles, this is clearly an organization that understands its relationship to others. Starbucks is another organization with strong ideals and a community and environmental focus. For example, their Environmental Footprint program involves a team of partners working together to ensure sustainability in sourcing, transportation, store design, and store operations. Their many active charitable programs, not to mention their unprecedented employee benefits, also illustrate their commitment to society.

Sticking to your ideals isn't always easy, especially amid pressure to compete. As Toyota grows internationally, they are finding it difficult to integrate their philosophies into production facilities around the world. Toyota is actively working to remedy the issue through the use of global training institutes. Starbucks faces growth-induced challenges as well. Some complain that the company's stated employee-focus hasn't proliferated to all of its stores. Others complain that Starbucks' high prices send a message of greed and that its size allows it to pay premium real estate prices with which smaller business can't compete. The company also faces frequent criticism for its empire mentality and is often viewed overseas as an example of U.S. cultural and economic imperialism. Even with regard to its strong social commitment, Starbucks faces challenges.

Starbucks, like other coffee roasters, has historically paid Ethiopian farmers between $1 and $2 per pound for their coffee beans, while one-pound bags of the same coffee sell for anywhere from $10 to $26 in the United States. To remedy this imbalance, the Ethiopian farmers began seeking to trademark their brands to gain better leverage in the marketplace. Initially, while Starbucks didn't exactly *support* the farmers in their trademark quest, it issued a joint statement with the Ethiopian government, stating that it would not oppose their efforts. After the plight of the Ethiopian farmers became public, more than 96,000 people around the world called on Starbucks to sign a licensing agreement with Ethiopia. To their credit, Starbucks responded by signing the licensing agreement and agreeing to work with Ethiopian farmers to make their dreams a reality.[3] This not only helps the farmers, but Ethiopia's economy as a whole. In the end, Starbucks did the right thing by listening to its customer base and supporting the public's—and its own—values.

Vince Kellen, the Vice President of Information Systems (IS) at DePaul University, was recently faced with the monumental task of upgrading the university's Enterprise Resource Management (ERP) system. Unlike many people in his position, he refused to bring in expensive outside consultants, opting instead to leverage his existing staff. Despite pressure from his demanding boss to bring instant results, Kellen took the time to build an agile organization, with rotating roles built around people's strengths. To deal with his tough boss, Kellen says, "I kept my list of goals in one pocket and my resignation letter in the other."[4] Fortunately, the resignation wasn't necessary, and the IS organization was successfully transformed. Kellen knew what he stood for and stuck by it.

Many companies craft fluffy mission statements, which are often ignored in the daily realities of work. Frequently, the sentiments that a company makes public have no bearing on how they operate internally on a day-to-day basis. Consider the words of Charles Dwyer:

> *Each person who gets involved [in the creation of a mission statement] is waiting to see whether or not the rewards and punishments, the allocation of resources, will actually bear any resemblance to what it was they got excited about, if they got excited about it in the first place. What they know is that it often won't.* [5]

As we've learned with Starbucks and Toyota, we must continuously self-reflect and adapt in order to ensure that our actions, and our employees' actions, support our ideals.

Leon Gorman, Chairman of L.L. Bean, knows what his company stands for. Day in and day out, L.L. Bean lives its values. Their high customer and employee satisfaction rates bear witness to this. More specifically, Gorman says:

> *[Our goal is to] completely fulfill our responsibilities to all our stakeholders... our customers, employees, management group, owners; our communities and our natural environment. And also our vendors... We do not believe in profit maximization or maximization of shareholder value. We believe in optimizing the value that we create, and we add to the lives of all our stakeholders. [Our goal is] adding to the quality of life of our customers through our product, service, and similarly, adding to the quality of life for our employees: in individual development, job security, and dealing with their aspirations.* [6]

As we discussed in Chapter 7, Ricardo Semler is another leader who knows what he stands for. His Semco organization lists democracy, transparency, and trust among its guiding principles. As Semler puts it, "In such a system the driving force of productivity is motivation and genuine interest, not predetermined routines and hulking foremen." [7] We've already learned about Semco's flexible environment in which people make their own hours. Other examples of tangible ways that Semco supports their principles are as follows:

- When people are hired or promoted, others in that unit interview and evaluate the candidates before a decision is made. Formal education is not viewed as a criterion for employment.
- A person can make more money than their manager, depending on specialized skill, experience, or a number of other factors. Salaries are not tied to job titles. In fact, there are very few job titles, period.
- Each business unit has a committee through which the employees in the unit can voice their interests. Potential conflict with Semco interests is viewed as healthy, and debate is encouraged.
- Leading by fear or disrespecting employees is not tolerated. Employees evaluate their managers anonymously twice a year on core values.
- Employees are encouraged to block out a half day a week for "thinking time." They're also encouraged to avoid meetings in favor of phone calls or hallway conversations where appropriate.
- Employees who meet at least 70 percent of the requirements for a new job are chosen over outsiders who may meet 100 percent of the requirements.
- Rules are kept to an absolute minimum. Policies, whether travel expense, security, or purchasing policies, are based on trust.[8]

Semco and the other "high-ideal" organizations we've highlighted seem to have taken to heart the wise words spoken by Albert Einstein:

*Concern for man and his fate must always form the chief
interest of all technical endeavors. Never forget this in the
midst of your diagrams and equations.*

As we can see by these examples, our ideals define who
we are and serve to guide our priorities, even in the face of
difficult challenges. If these ideals are spread throughout
the organization and are used to guide everyday decisions
(as opposed to simply being lip service), they enable us
to ease up on the rulebook "foot pedal." That's when real
growth happens.

One software product that can aid in diagnosing
misalignment in an organization's culture and values is
Infotool (www.infotool-online.com). More than just a
survey tool, it allows senior executives to visualize their
organization's strengths and weaknesses—and where its
values may be out of synch—by functional group, management level, geography, and a whole host of other demographics. It also shows where intervention may be needed
and offers navigation paths for targeted improvements. The
product is fairly new, but has thus far received rave reviews
from its A-list clientele as perhaps the only tool on the market geared toward facilitating shared ideals.

Leading by Questioning

Even with the strongest of ideals, there will be times
when we are faced with challenges so difficult that we
question who we really are. Consider the case of a poorly-
performing employee who is having personal problems at
home with a sick parent or child, or a company directive
that goes against your very moral fiber. Consider having to
make a decision that is ethically sound but will decrease
shareholder value in the short term. For cases such as these,
there is no mission statement, value statement, or policy

manual in the world that will contain the undisputed "right" answer. Even personal ethics alone aren't adequate, as there is a whole system to consider.

A recent *Business Week* article highlighted a controversy over Hershey, the Pennsylvania-based chocolate company. Hershey has been around for more than 100 years and has been a core part of its community, with its themed hotels, amusement parks, and even its chocolate-themed influences on local street lamps and street signs. It built its reputation on providing low-cost, high-quality chocolate, using local workers and products from local farmers. Five years ago, the board of a $5 billion charitable trust that controls Hershey tried to sell the organization. Pennsylvania Attorney General D. Michael Fisher challenged the sale, since a new owner would likely move jobs out of state. Under pressure, the board backed down. Now that Hershey's CEO, Richard Lenny, has announced that he'll be retiring this year, the issue has resurfaced. Two law professors recently wrote that the trust made a mistake in not selling the company, as it destroyed an estimated $2.7 billion in shareholder value.[9]

What should take precedence in this case—Hershey's community-based ideals or shareholder value? What if we also consider that Hershey recently had to raise prices, shut down at least one plant, and cut more than 1,500 jobs because of the rising cost of cocoa butter, corn syrup, and packaging? Or that their attempts to try new products, such as organic and dark chocolate, haven't succeeded? Does that change anything?

Joseph Badaracco calls these "defining moments" in his book of the same title. According to Badaracco, these issues serve to "reveal, test, and shape" who we are and who we are to become.[10] In meeting this challenge, we cannot look to a guidebook for a quick solution. We need to make some tough decisions.

A popular paradox called *Buridan's Ass* (named for four-teenth-century French philosopher, Jean Buridan) states that an otherwise rational donkey, when placed between two equally appealing stacks of hay, will starve to death because it cannot make a rational decision. Centuries earlier, Aristotle told of a man who could not decide between food and drink. To this day, people struggle with making decisions, especially when dealing with gray areas.

There are numerous decision-making tools and processes. More than 200 years ago, Benjamin Franklin devised a decision-making model that involved listing the advantages and disadvantages of each option. In the 1960s, Drs. Charles Kepner and Benjamin Tregoe created a fancier model for the U.S. Air Force (called Kepner-Tregoe), which involves assessing the situation, ranking and weighting targeted objectives, generating alternatives, scoring the alternatives based on the objectives, and comparing benefits and risks to select the best alternative. John Hammond, Howard Raiffa, and Ralph Keeney created a method called *Even Swaps*, in which values are placed on each alternative, and offsetting items are crossed out. Author Edward De Bono suggests we rate items for each alternative as "plus, minus, or interesting" and total up the scores. These are but a few of many decision-making models. Yet they are of limited value when faced with equally compelling truths. Instead, we must ask the right questions.

In Chapter 3, we explored Arthur Dobrin's eight-step process for integrating virtue ethics, consequentialist [results-based] ethics, and principled ethics. His process ensures that we examine the facts, our feelings, the values that are important to us, and the potential consequences of our actions.[11]

In the book *Asking the Right Questions: A Guide to Critical Thinking*, authors M. Neil Browne and Stuart M. Keeley propose that we identify any words or phrases that may be ambiguous, what assumptions are held by all parties, what fallacies may exist in the reasoning, and what significant information is omitted. They also suggest asking what value conflicts may be present.[12]

When value conflicts exist, one of the best lists of questions I've come across is Joseph Badaracco's. Among the many crucial questions included in his book, the following are particularly relevant, and often overlooked:

- Which of the responsibilities and values in conflict have the deepest roots in my life and in communities I care about?
- How can expediency and shrewdness, along with imagination and boldness, move me toward the goals I care about most strongly? [Also assuming that one needs to pick one's battles wisely.]
- What is the cash value [i.e., the value-satisfier] of this situation and of my ideas for the people whose support I need?
- Have I done all I can to secure my position and the strength and stability of my organization?
- Have I thought creatively and imaginatively about my organization's role in society and its relationship to stakeholders?
- What allies do I have inside and outside my company?
- Which parties will resist or fight my efforts? Have I underestimated their power and tactical skill or overestimated their ethics?
- Have I done all I can to strike a balance, both morally and practically?
- What ethical values have the managers whom I know and admire chosen as guides for their organizations?

- What managers, in my experience, have thought creatively and imaginatively about their organization's role in society and its responsibility to stakeholders?[13]

The concept of "leading by questioning" is not new. The father of this approach was Socrates, whose probing methods to encourage his pupils to think deeper are used to this day, especially in the education and legal fields. According to critical thinking expert Richard Paul, Socrates addressed six types of questions to his pupils. The six types, and some representative examples, are as follows:

Types of Questions	Examples
Questions for clarification	• Why are you saying that? • What exactly does this mean, and can you give me an example?
Questions that probe assumptions	• You seem to be assuming...? How did you choose those assumptions? • What else could we assume? What would happen if...?
Questions that probe reason and evidence	• Why do you think this is happening? What do you think causes...? • How do you know this? Can you show me or give me an example? • What evidence is there to support what you are saying?

Types of Questions	Examples
Questions about viewpoints and perspectives	• What alternative ways of looking at this are there? • What are the pros and cons of...? • What would...say about it?
Questions that probe implications and consequences	• Then what would happen? • What are the consequences of that assumption? • How could...be used to...? How does...affect...?
Questions about the question	• What was the point of asking that question? • Is that the right question?

14

By asking such questions instead of jumping to conclusions and adopting quick-fix solutions, we can be more prepared to navigate the gray areas. As for Hershey's dilemma, if we were in charge, we could easily use these questions to probe those who feel that selling the company would be the best solution as well as those who oppose the option. Likewise, we could use the other questions we've introduced (which were all in some way inspired by Socrates) to probe our own personal feelings and values. We could address the question, "Whom do we serve?" And we could look for creative solutions to meet the needs of all parties (including addressing Hershey's financial woes). Ultimately, we could use these questions to test—and possibly reevaluate—who we are and what we stand for.

In cases of right versus right, there is no correct answer. There is only the answer that will define who we are, and who our organization or team will become; the answer that will best integrate virtue ethics, consequentialist ethics, and principled ethics. In order to arrive at this answer, it is vital that we ask the right questions.

Systems Thinking

Although the concept of systems thinking has been around since antiquity (Aristotle coined the phrase, "The whole is more than the sum of its parts"), Peter Senge's *The Fifth Discipline* raised its popularity to new heights when the book was released in 1990. Systems thinking is essential for understanding complex problems, and thus of great use when managing the gray areas.

Instead of a traditional "cause and effect" model, in which factors A, B, and C might affect D, a systems model looks at A, B, C, and D independently and together, in different variations; in essence, the *relationships* of A, B, C, and D. The model also examines external factors that might otherwise have gone overlooked. Systems thinking assumes that one cannot understand the whole just by looking at its parts. One must look at the whole, including relationships and external factors.[15]

Systems thinking is also the realm of quantum physics, or the "new science," as Meg Wheatley describes (I've added the underlines):

> One of the first differences between new science and Newtonianism is a focus on holism rather than parts. Systems are understood as whole systems, and attention is given to <u>relationships within those networks</u>. Donella Meadows, an ecologist and author, quotes an ancient Sufi teaching that captures this shift in focus: "You think because you understand <u>one</u> you must understand <u>two</u>, because one and one makes two. But you must also understand <u>and</u>."[16]

Understanding *and* is the essence of systems thinking.

There are a number of approaches and tools that can help us in our efforts to leverage systems thinking:

- Meg Wheatley advises that we always include a broad diversity of people in our endeavors, to offset biases. The group doesn't necessarily have to be large, but it should represent a broad array of viewpoints.[17]

- Models such as Appreciative Inquiry (AI) can be used to identify the collective strengths of an organization and build upon them to create a new future. A key element of AI is that the "whole system" must be present. This also takes strengths-based management to an organizational level.

- Neuro-Linguistic Programming (NLP) teaches us how to use all of our senses (i.e., the "whole system") to give us more holistic views and help us communicate better to others. Its premise is that people act and feel based on their limited perceptions of the world around them.

- Fons Trompenaars and Charles Hampden-Turner suggest that instead of comparing two extremes, we should examine them in a circular fashion, exploring the impacts each one has on the other.[18]

- Related to this, Causal Loop Diagrams (CLDs) allow us to list, in a spiral fashion, the related elements of a problem, how they behave over time, and what interactions or factors might induce change. Examples can be found at Pegasus Communications' Systems Thinker Web site: http://www.thesystemsthinker.com/tstgdlines2.html.

- Software, such as *Stella* and *iThink* from iSee Systems (http://www.iseesystems.com) allows us to map out complex systems, create process models, and examine the impact of hypothetical changes over time. Mindjet's *MindManager* software is another excellent tool for brainstorming and mapping relationships.

- The Six Sigma process begins with building a Suppliers, Inputs, Processes, Outputs, Customers (SIPOC) diagram to ensure that the "whole system" is considered in process design and problem resolution. There are plenty of SIPOC templates available at no charge on the Internet.

All of these approaches focus on understanding the whole system through its relationships. Perhaps the best example of this is Peter Scholtes' interpretation of Knute Rockne's famous "Win one for the Gipper" motivational speech:

> *Didn't Knute Rockne motivate the Fighting Irish, in his stirring half time speech, to "win one for the Gipper"? The never-asked alternative question: "Would Notre Dame have won the game without the speech?" I submit that what won the game was the training, conditioning, and coaching that began years before the fateful game. The system won the game, not the oratory. But my version, I admit, would not have made as good a movie.*[19]

Without systems thinking, we make shallow assumptions and near-sighted decisions because we overlook important impacts and relationships.

There is inherent danger in only looking at the parts of a system. This is especially true when designing incentives. For example, in Michael Hammer and James Champy's book *Reengineering the Corporation*, they tell the story of a multimillion dollar jet that sat idle because the maintenance man's boss wouldn't send him to fix it until the next day, to avoid paying for a hotel stay.[20] The boss' incentives were geared toward the tight budget of his own unit, to the disservice of the company as a whole. In the health care industry, misguided incentives frequently lead doctors, hospitals, insurance companies, and drug providers away from focusing on patient outcomes and the patient experience. There are countless examples of employees trying to make a quota or win a prize, to the detriment of the organization. Incentives can actually drive the elements of a system to work against each other instead of together. To remedy this, we need to ask: What's the primary purpose of the system as a whole? (This ties back to our choice to "stand for something.")

We also need to focus on causes, not just results. As Peter Scholtes cautions us, "Measurable goals do not improve systems; accountability does not improves systems. *Improving systems* improves systems." To this, he adds,

> *Do people need to be accountable? Of course they do. And they are, almost all the time! The question, therefore, is mostly irrelevant. A better question is: Why do things go wrong even when those doing the work are being accountable and doing their best?* [21]

We must observe a few cautions when examining whole systems. Try as we might, we can never fully understand the complete system, including all its relationships and potential causes. As we learned in Chapter 9, relationships are often unseen and thus unpredictable. The map is not the territory. We can only *approximate* the truth. We can get close by mapping what we know, and observing and gathering evidence. Pfeffer and Sutton's "evidence-based management" approach is an excellent model to follow. On their Web site (http://www.evidence-basedmanagement.com), they offer the five principles of evidence-based management, which serve to support a systems thinking model:

1. Face the hard facts, and build a culture in which people are encouraged to tell the truth, even if it is unpleasant.

2. Be committed to "fact-based" decision making—
   which means being committed to getting the best
   evidence and using it to guide actions.

3. Treat your organization as an unfinished
   prototype—encourage experimentation and
   learning by doing.

4. Look for the risks and drawbacks in what people
   recommend—even the best medicine has side
   effects.

5. Avoid basing decisions on untested but strongly
   held beliefs, what you have done in the past, or on
   uncritical "benchmarking" of what winners do.[22]

Another issue when engaging in systems thinking (and
something that an evidence-based approach would help us
avoid), is the temptation to assume that a software product will substitute for, or drive, "the system." For example,
as a recent *CIO Magazine* article pointed out, an Enterprise
Resource Planning (ERP) system can help support com-
pliance with enterprise policies and drive standardization.[23] However, on the down side, a data problem in one
area infiltrates the whole data pool, and local flexibility is
curtailed as well, as a result of the system's enforcement
of globally mandated processes. The company is wound
together like a chain gang, unable to leverage individualism.
Who knows what impact this may have on productivity
and employee morale, or which factors may raise implementation costs beyond any value gained? Perhaps this
is why 51 percent of ERP initiatives are reported to have
failed.[24] Undoubtedly, shared information is a vital element
of any successful organization. Still, when it comes to ERP
software, we need to ask: Are there alternative ways to
spread best practices? Are there other methods available for
gaining global visibility of information, such as integrated
best-of-breed software? Is there a more holistic solution

that considers the human element and allows for flexibility? Given the evidence, these are questions worth asking.

We cannot forget that people, and the ways in which they relate to one another, are major elements of any system. Their beliefs and biases are a very real part of everyday activities. The human element cannot be ignored.

This brings us to our fourth and final theme of gray area management—empathy and cultural awareness.

Empathy and Cultural Awareness

Empathy, or the ability to put yourself in someone else's shoes, is a key factor in *Emotional Intelligence*, a term coined by Daniel Goleman in his book of the same name. Empathy is also central to the ability to influence people. From organizational change to world conflicts, empathy has been proven to be a powerful element in problem avoidance and resolution. As Goleman notes:

> *If your emotional abilities aren't in hand, if you don't have self-awareness, if you are not able to manage your distressing emotions, if you can't have empathy and have effective relationships, then no matter how smart you are, you are not going to get very far.*

A key element of empathy is the ability to understand cultural differences. Cultural differences can exist across multiple geographies, functions, organizations, or ethnic backgrounds. For instance, someone from the United States, Germany, or England might be more inclined to be rule-oriented, whereas someone from one of the Asian or Latin countries might be more flexible. An American may be frustrated when he or she arrives promptly to meet someone from Spain or Latin America, only to find that those cultures do not have such a precise view of time. In Japan, there is a strong need to save face, so people may be less apt to risk voicing their opinions in meetings. Even certain business functions, such as marketing or engineering, carry their own cultures. Some companies have a strong culture that pervades the entire organization.

Building cultural awareness does not happen overnight. There is a maturity path we must follow. Stephanie Quappe and Giovanna Cantatore have an excellent article on the Culturosity Web site, titled "What is Cultural Awareness Anyway? How Do I Build It?" In the article, they propose that there are four degrees of cultural awareness, as follows:

Degrees of Cultural Awareness	Description
My way is the only way (Parochial stage)	People are only aware of their way of doing things, and feel that their way is the only way.
I know their way, but my way is better (Ethnocentric stage)	People are aware of other ways of doing things, but still consider their way as the best one. They ignore or minimize the other ways.
My way and their way (Synergistic stage)	People are aware of their own way of doing things and others' ways of doing things, and they choose the best method according to the situation.
Our way (Participatory Third Culture stage)	People from different cultural backgrounds work together in the creation of a culture of shared meanings. There is open dialogue, and new meanings and rules are created.

25

Culture isn't the only differentiator with which we must be concerned. Differences exist between genders as well. For example, women are more inclined to be aware of relationships and practices when solving problems. They are typically less concerned about the end game than they are about the process of getting there. Men are more concerned about winning and solving the puzzle and are less apt to include others. With regard to focus, women tend to take in everything at once, simultaneously thinking in multiple directions, while men tend to focus on one thing at a time. When recalling past events, women remember things by their emotional ties, whereas men try to reconstruct events based on observations of activities at the time. With relationships, women tend to relate to others through open dialogue and sharing of emotions, whereas men best relate to others through shared experiences. All of these are general tendencies, not certainties.

Supporting these findings, however, are a number of studies, including one led by psychology professor Richard Haier and neuropsychologist Rex Jung. The study, performed at the University of New Mexico, showed that, during IQ tests, men mostly used the gray matter in their brains (which represents the information processing centers), and women mostly used the white matter (which connects these processing centers). As Jung explains, this may be why women may have an inclination toward thinking more holistically.[26]

Despite the differences in thought processing and brain physiology (ironically, men have slightly more white matter on average, even though they primarily use the gray matter, and vice-versa for women), the genders fare equally in IQ tests.[27] Can recognizing these differences and tendencies impact our understanding of one another or enable us to leverage each other's natural abilities? It is helpful to be aware of such traits, but we need to be careful. As Jung points out, despite the clear differences in the ways men and women use gray and white matter to process information, overall brain function depends partly on genetics (which, to a degree, are environmentally determined), and the social and cultural interactions of the individual.

One might say these thoughts on gender and culture are tantamount to generalizing, and they'd be absolutely right. There is an important difference, however, between generalizing, which uses certain assumptions as a *starting point*, versus stereotyping, which uses those assumptions as the *ending point*. To generalize as a starting point, when those generalizations are supported by research, is appropriate, provided we use them to try to understand, and not to judge, others. We also need to do this with the knowledge that every individual is unique, and thus may "go against the grain." Who's to say whether a person's country, gender, social influences, ethnic background, or functional or organizational influences will take precedence?

When trying to understand someone else's perspective, despite hints we may glean from his or her gender and/ or culture, we must also be able to *sense* what he or she is feeling. We can gain a further understanding with queries, clarifications, and responses, such as:

Queries
- Can you tell me more about that?
- What has this been like for you?
- How has all of this made you feel?

Clarifications:
- Let me see if I've gotten this right...
- Tell me more about...
- I want to make sure I understand what you've said...

Responses:
- Sounds like you are...
- I imagine that must be...
- I can understand that must make you feel...[28]

We must also be aware of people's individual preferences, which may or may not be related to their culture or gender. For instance, people have individual communication preferences (visual, auditory, kinesthetic, etc.). While e-mail may be effective with one person, a face-to-face meeting might work best with another. While one person may prefer descriptive text, another may prefer pictures and graphs. While one person may prefer experiential learning, another may prefer to understand the details first. For this reason, it is often best to communicate using multiple methods. There are many rules of thumb regarding when to send e-mails and when to meet in person, but for every rule there's an exception. For example, if we want to communicate a complex message, an e-mail memo can allow someone to organize and digest the information slowly, yet a face-to-face interaction can communicate the message in broader context, and with the support of nonverbal communication. A solution might be to send an e-mail message and follow up with an in-person conversation, or vice-versa, depending on the situation. The bottom line is that we need to understand our audiences and their preferences.

Another way in which we must understand our audience is to be cognizant of people's perceived gains and losses regarding anything we need them to support. Their values may not be the same as ours, so it would be unwise to assume we know what motivates them. Formulating what we think others are feeling based on our own paradigms is a dangerous road to travel. We need to observe George Bernard Shaw's cautionary statement:

Do not do unto others as you would that they should do unto you. Their tastes may not be the same.

Let's look at one last example in which empathy is relevant—performance appraisals. The problem with performance appraisals can be attributed to two reasonably safe assumptions. First, people generally do not like being judged by anyone they feel isn't qualified to judge them. Second, most people feel they are above average. If we accept these assumptions to be true, a more effective approach might be to provide ongoing, timely, specific, and less formal feedback.

In the book *Abolishing Performance Appraisals,* Tom Coens and Mary Jenkins tell of how General Motors' GM-Powertrain division experimented with better ways to evaluate employees. They began with a 360-degree feedback system that was nonquantitative in nature, only to find that people still didn't like it. No matter how it was sliced, people still didn't like being judged. After further research, they tried a new program. Employees were educated on the benefits of feedback and were given a mechanism by which they could solicit feedback from others of their choosing. This could be done on an ongoing basis as needed and was entirely at the employee's discretion. Managers were not involved unless asked by the employee. There was no formal appraisal process. This new model resulted in a 50 percent adoption rate and higher employee engagement overall. The system is now being used in many departments at General Motors.[29]

As the authors note, some may claim that appraisals are required in order to adhere to certain regulations. To conform to such regulations, many companies use a checklist to document that requisite conversations or meetings were held with employees.

Coens and Jenkins also reference a statement from Jim McIngvale, owner of the Gallery Furniture Company in Houston, Texas, that illustrates this humanistic mentality:

> *We appraise people every day as they need it. We talk to people and listen to them. We try to give people jobs and tasks they like*

to do. We help them if they need it, but mostly we try to make work fun. Work is supposed to be fun. Appraisals get in the way of this. We're in the customer business, not the appraisal business! Ninety percent of people will be disappointed with appraisals because they all expect top ratings.[30]

Some might ask: What should be done when workers appear to be abusing the system or simply aren't performing? If we focus on outcomes and address Bud Bilanich's eleven reasons for fixing performance problems (which we referred to in Chapter 3), we'll discover, in many cases, that the system is at fault and not the person. There will always be abusers. They represent the minority and should be treated as the exception, not the rule. There will also be those who need coaching, and by all means, they should be coached. Yet organizations would be wise to examine their appraisal processes and the results they are supposed to generate, and ask themselves, "Is this the best way to achieve these results?"

Overall, as we can see from our exploration of the four themes of gray area management, if we have strong ideals, and our organization lives and breathes those ideals; if we lead by questioning, never to assume anything at face value; if we employ systems thinking to understand the influence of relationships and external factors; and if we apply empathy and cultural awareness to all we do, we can rise to a higher level of leadership and make a difference in this ever-evolving world. And, even if we are not at the helm of our organization, we can still each do our part to spread the important concept of gray thinking. As leaders, we are in a unique position to do so.

Key Concepts

- Knowing what we stand for can provide much-needed clarity when making decisions, guiding our priorities in the face of daily stress.

- For issues of "right versus right," mission statements, value statements, and policy manuals cannot help. Even personal ethics and traditional decision-making models offer limited value. We need to ask better questions, such as those proposed in this chapter.

- Systems thinking states that we cannot understand the whole just by looking at its parts. We must look at the whole, including relationships and external factors.

- The concepts and tools offered in this chapter, such as Appreciative Inquiry, Neuro-Linguistic Programming, Causal Loop Diagrams, SIPOC, and specialized software like iSee Systems' *Stella* and *iThink* and Mindjet's *MindManager* are valuable in helping leaders to facilitate systems thinking.

- Opposite approaches must be examined in terms of their impact on one another, not as separate concepts.

- Many incentives can actually drive the elements of a system to work against each other instead of together.

- The map is not the territory. Relationships are often unseen and thus unpredictable. Even with systems thinking, we can only *approximate* the truth.

- We can improve our odds of predictability by using evidence-based management, as endorsed by Jeffrey Pfeffer and Bob Sutton.

- A whole system includes people, their beliefs and norms, and external factors. A software product cannot substitute for, or drive, "the system."

- To foster empathy, it is beneficial to understand the cultural differences that exist across multiple geographies, functions, organizations, genders, or ethnic backgrounds.

- Understanding cultural differences can be used as a *starting point* for considering relationship factors, but should never be assumed to be the *ending point.* People's behaviors are influenced by many other factors, including genetics, social interactions, and other life experiences.

- In displaying empathy, we must also be aware of people's communication preferences and their perceived gains and/or losses regarding issues with which we seek their support.

- Through empathy, we can understand why performance appraisals often do not achieve results: People generally do not like being judged by anyone they feel isn't qualified to judge them, and most people feel they are above average. Ongoing, timely, specific, and less formal feedback may be more productive.

? Questions to Ponder

1. What does my organization stand for? What do I stand for? Are there discrepancies? How can I use the questions in this chapter to resolve them?

2. How can I use the tools in this chapter to encourage systems thinking and focus on the whole instead of the parts?

3. Are there incentives in my group that work against the organization as a whole?

4. Can I make a better effort to understand others through learning about their culture or individual preferences? How can I put myself in their shoes and not interject my view of the world? How can I look at things through *their* eyes?

Notes

Get even more from this book. Visit **www.rmcpublications.com/grayareas** to share your thoughts and questions on topics in this chapter and to access additional resources.

Chapter 11
Preparing for Gray Area Success

"The leader of the past knew how to tell. The leader of the future will know how to ask."

‑ Peter Drucker

Thus far, we've explored a number of topics in our study of the seven gray areas most leaders face. We've examined ways to simultaneously meet individual and organizational needs. We've seen how to leverage generalists and specialists, and how to communicate with simplicity and context. We've discussed how to operate on the edge of chaos, and how to practice situational leadership. We've discovered that appearance and substance both matter, and that decentralized organizations can prosper if held together by shared ideals and information. Finally, we've seen how, with the core themes of knowing what we stand for, leading by questioning, systems thinking, and empathy and cultural awareness, we can better navigate through life's tough challenges.

From these collective lessons and themes, we can derive six fundamental principles that can serve as our compass when managing the gray areas:

1. Strive to blend opposing concepts or values
2. Understand the relationship between all things
3. Question judiciously

4. Never assume one size fits all
5. Leverage collective intelligence
6. Favor freedom

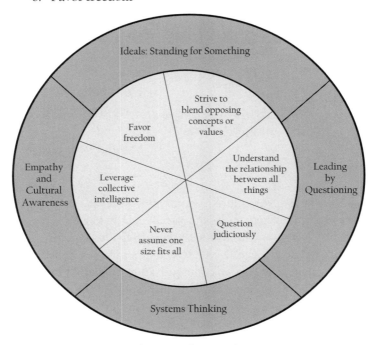

Themes and Principles

Groucho Marx once said, "Here are my principles, and if you don't like them...well, I have others." Although it's a humorous comment, in reality there are many principles that can guide us in our lives. It's up to each of us to discover what works for us in the context of who we are and to whom we are connected. While universal principles should be used with caution (much harm has been done in the name of firm principles), the previous list can help trigger gray thinking. Think of it as a checklist of reminders. Put the reminders in your PDA, or tape them to your wall.

Add your own principles that help you achieve gray thinking. Add your favorite tips from this book and from others. Refer to it often. You'll find that, little by little, your habits will begin to change and you'll begin looking at issues from broader perspectives. You'll begin asking pointed questions and challenging others to do the same. You might even find yourself reevaluating your priorities. That's when you'll know that growth lies ahead.

As F. Scott Fitzgerald said, "Vitality shows in not only the ability to persist, but the ability to start over."

Making a Difference

Some people may read this book and feel they're not in a position to implement many of the ideas. This is a common complaint among those in middle management. In some cases, they are correct. Many changes, however, can be made on a small scale, which can ultimately have a big impact. One only need look at Best Buy, where the Results-Only Work Environment sprouted from a grass-roots beginning. Fortunately, anyone can benefit from gray thinking. We must all do our part within the context in which we are operating.

In many ways, the middle management layer of an organization is the most important. That's where the true culture of an organization is often set, not at the lofty, visionary layers. I recently heard someone refer to middle management as the "Jell-O layer," because that's where everything gets stuck between senior management and the workers (both from a top-down and bottom-up perspective). It's an apt description. Yet by adopting new practices and spreading new ideas, middle managers can foster powerful change. They can make a difference.

As leaders at any level, we need to challenge the status quo. We need to ask probing questions and reexamine our priorities. Even the examples we've seen in this book warrant further questioning. For example, does culture play a role in Semco's success with such an open philosophy? Could the same approach work without a committed leader at the very top of the organization? What elements contribute to the success of the Results-Only Work Environment at Best Buy, in addition to its focus on results and its flexible approach? What commonalities exist in other organizations using the model? Can the model sustain its excellent track record with employee engagement, or is it like the Hawthorne effect, where workers are engaged because they're being studied? Does it take a certain type of employee to thrive in such an environment? I raise these questions even as I offer these initiatives as shining examples of humane leadership and enlightened thinking.

I can't begin to count the number of organizations in which I've heard the words, "It won't work here because we're different." Sometimes that's a true statement, but oftentimes it's not. We must examine the evidence and, if feasible, try it out on a small scale. We may find that we like certain elements of an approach, but not others. Again, we must try it out to be sure the approach can still work with some of its elements missing. We must also remember to secure broad representation in any pilot program we undertake, as there are invisible elements that can impact success. The more diverse the pilot group, the likelier our pilot will be valid.

These are just a few examples of gray area thinking at work. With this mindset, when someone asks us to comment on a new document or form, we can respond with a two-part question: Who is the audience, and what are they supposed to do with the information? If someone asks us to implement a process, we can ask questions such as: What problem is this supposed to solve, and why do you believe this will solve it? What assumptions are being made that may not be valid? Who can we include in order to gain multiple perspectives?

If we're fortunate enough to be at the helm of our organization, we can challenge ourselves, asking: What if the primary currency of our organization weren't time or money, but relationships and shared goals? Organizations are making huge profits with this very philosophy.

The Path Forward: Our Role as Leaders

We began our journey with the caveat that, while we cannot guarantee *right* answers, we can ensure that we arrive at *thoughtful* answers. We can approximate the truth, but that is all. Knowing this, we cannot lose heart if we do not achieve perfection. Perfection is not the goal—excellence is.

Long-term organizational excellence requires learning. And learning involves mistakes and disruptive change. That is how we grow. To succumb to short-term pressures and to strive for the illusion of perfection is to deny that growth. In essence, our journey as leaders should be toward further growth, not to an imaginary finish line. In the Jewish ethical classic, *Pirkei Avot* (Ethics of the Fathers), Rabbi Tarfon said of perfecting the world, "It is not upon you to complete the work, but nor are you free to desist from it." These are wise words for any leader. They remind us that, whatever our role, we can make a difference.

Sometimes the road seems insurmountable. My friend Randall Goodman once shared a memory of the long drives he used to take to the mountains with his family. The sight of a "mountain range" on the horizon would give the impression that the destination was just ahead. Then, as they approached, it would turn out to be a set of hills. As they passed that set of hills, another set of hills would appear on the horizon. After a number of "false mountain ranges," he felt they'd never arrive. We spoke of how life sometimes mirrors that feeling. Yet, as Randall reminded me, each hill we pass, each challenge we meet, is behind us, and gets us one step closer. But closer to what?

Unlike Randall's trip, the mountain, when it appears, isn't our ultimate destination. It represents a new paradigm that, once we've reached it, becomes a peak from which we can see the next mountain. It is then that we are operating on a higher plateau. To reach this plateau, it is my sincere wish that you will join me in making a lifelong commitment to understanding—and managing—the gray areas. Let's make a commitment to maintaining an open mind, asking the right questions, and understanding our relationship to others. Let's strive to reevaluate what we stand for, and to see our part in the big picture. Let's agree to lead *through* people, and not *at* people. Then, we can all meet on the mountain and plot our next course. I hope to see you there.

Resources and Further Reading

The effort to improve gray thinking should not end with this book. On the contrary, this book is meant to serve as a primer, and to plant a seed that will lead to further growth. The ten books listed below, which served as a great inspiration to me, can help with that growth. They include a wealth of examples and case studies that can provide a better understanding of the gray areas. When it comes to opening your mind, here are "ten for the road":

1. *21 Leaders for the 21st Century: How Innovative Leaders Manage in the Digital Age* by Fons Trompenaars and Charles Hampden-Turner

2. *Good Business: Leadership, Flow, and the Making of Meaning* by Mihaly Csikszentmihalyi

3. *Hard Facts, Dangerous Half-Truths, and Total Nonsense: Profiting from Evidence-Based Management* by Jeffrey Pfeffer and Robert I. Sutton

4. *Maverick: The Success Story Behind the World's Most Unusual Workplace* by Ricardo Semler

5. *Defining Moments: When Managers Must Choose between Right and Right* by Joseph L. Badaracco, Jr.

6. *Leadership and the New Science: Discovering Order in a Chaotic World* by Margaret Wheatley

7. *The DNA of Leadership: Leverage Your Instincts to Communicate, Differentiate, Innovate* by Judith E. Glaser

8. *First, Break All the Rules: What the World's Greatest Managers Do Differently* by Marcus Buckingham and Curt Coffman

9. *The Leader's Handbook: Making Things Happen, Getting Things Done* by Peter R. Scholtes

10. *The Starfish and the Spider: The Unstoppable Power of Leaderless Organizations* by Ori Brafman and Rod Beckstrom

As for other gray area resources, there are books that I've referenced in the bibliography, as well as a number of organizations that are dedicated to understanding multiple perspectives, including:

- The Caux Round Table Principles for Business (http://www.cauxroundtable.org)
- The Global Integrity Alliance (https://www.integrityalliance.org)
- The Institute for Ethics and Emerging Technologies (http://ieet.org)
- The International Institute for Public Ethics (http://www.iipe.org)

I wish you well on your quest to discovering the gray areas.

Notes

Chapter 1

1. Reprinted by permission of *Harvard Business School Press*.
   From *Hard Facts, Dangerous Half-Truths, and Total Nonsense: Profiting from Evidence-Based Management* by Jeffrey Pfeffer and Robert I. Sutton. Boston, MA 2006, p 52.
   Copyright © 2006, by the Harvard Business School Publishing Corporation, all rights reserved.

2. Ram Charan, "Five Rules for Setting the Right Priorities," Yahoo! Finance, April 11, 2007, http://finance.yahoo. com/expert/article/companyknow/29003.

3. Ibid.

Chapter 2

1. Fons Trompenaars, *Did the Pedestrian Die? Insights from the World's Greatest Culture Guru* (Oxford: Capstone Publishing Limited, 2003), pp 1-2.

2. Ibid, pp 2-3, 5.

3. Ibid, pp 6, 68.

4. Jim Collins and Jerry I. Porras, *Built to Last: Successful Habits of Visionary Companies* (New York: Collins, 2002).

5. Bruce Thompson, "Fallacy Page," Cuyamaca College, http:// www.cuyamaca.edu/brucethompson/Fallacies/intro_fallacies. asp.

6. Bruce Thompson, "Black & White Thinking," Cuyamaca College, http://www.cuyamaca.edu/brucethompson/Fallacies/ black&white.asp.

7. Ibid.

8. Dennis Littky and Samantha Grabelle, *The Big Picture: Education Is Everyone's Business* (Alexandria, VA: Association for Supervision and Curriculum Development, 2004), p 29.

9. Ibid, pp 43, 44.

10. Phil Rosenzweig, *The Halo Effect... And the Eight Other Business Delusions That Deceive Managers* (New York: Free Press, 2007), p 10.

11. Reprinted by permission of *Harvard Business School Press.* From *Hard Facts, Dangerous Half-Truths, and Total Nonsense: Profiting from Evidence-Based Management* by Jeffrey Pfeffer and Robert I. Sutton. Boston, MA 2006, pp 35, 107, 108. Copyright © 2006, by the Harvard Business School Publishing Corporation, all rights reserved.

12. Byron Williams, "Black and White Thinking Doesn't Work in a Gray World," *The Huffington Post*, October 2, 2006, http://www.huffingtonpost.com/byron-williams/black-and-white-thinking-_b_30747.html.

13. Ibid.

14. Ibid.

15. Carmine Coyote, "Seeing in Black and White," Slow Leadership, August 16, 2006, http://www.slowleadership.org/2006/08/seeing-in-black-and-white.html.

16. Ibid.

17. Uncommon Knowledge, Ltd., "All or Nothing Thinking," Depression Learning Path, http://www.clinical-depression.co.uk/Understanding_Depression/all_nothing.htm.

18. Ibid.

19. Charles Dwyer, *The Shifting Sources of Power and Influence* (Tampa, FL: American College of Physician Executives, 1991).

Chapter 3

1. Dwyer, *The Shifting Sources of Power and Influence.*

2. Marcus Buckingham and Curt Coffman, *First, Break All the Rules: What the World's Greatest Managers Do Differently* (New York: Simon & Schuster, 1999), p 59.

3. Buckingham and Coffman, *First, Break All the Rules.*

4. Arthur Dobrin, *Ethics for Everyone: How to Increase Your Moral Intelligence* (New York: J. Wiley & Sons, 2002), pp 21-22.

5. Ibid, pp 23-26.

6. Ibid, pp 31-32.

7. Bud Bilanich, *Fixing Performance Problems: Common Sense Ideas That Work* (Charleston, SC: BookSurge Publishing, 2005), p 5.

8. Reprinted by permission of *Harvard Business School Press*. From *Hard Facts, Dangerous Half-Truths, and Total Nonsense: Profiting from Evidence-Based Management* by Jeffrey Pfeffer and Robert I. Sutton. Boston, MA 2006, p 101. Copyright © 2006, by the Harvard Business School Publishing Corporation, all rights reserved.

9. John C. Maxwell, *The 360 Degree Leader: Developing Your Influence from Anywhere in the Organization* (Nashville: Thomas Nelson, 2006).

10. Hal F. Rosenbluth and Diane McFerrin Peters, *The Customer Comes Second: Put Your People First and Watch 'Em Kick Butt* (New York: Harper Business, 2002), p 10.

11. Ibid.

12. Keith Merron, *Consulting Mastery: How the Best Make the Biggest Difference* (San Francisco: Berrett-Koehler Publishers, 2005), p 75.
    Note: As a consultant, I typically use the term *client* instead of *customer*, as does Keith Merron in his book. Generally, a client is someone you help solve problems for, while a customer is someone who buys things from you. To address a variety of organizations, I've used the word *customer* in this book.

13. Merron, *Consulting Mastery*.

14. Patrick Lencioni, *Silos, Politics, and Turf Wars: A Leadership Fable About Destroying the Barriers That Turn Colleagues into Competitors* (San Francisco: Jossey-Bass, 2006), pp 178, 182, 186.

15. Judith E. Glaser, *The DNA of Leadership: Leverage Your Instincts to Communicate, Differentiate, Innovate* (Avon, MA: Platinum Press, 2006).

Chapter 4

1. Rosenbluth and McFerrin Peters, *The Customer Comes Second*, p 144.

2. Fred Nickols, "Generalist or Specialist: Which Do I Consult?" *Distance Consulting*, 2003, http://www.nickols.us.

3. Ibid.

4. M. Eric Johnson, "Put People Before Processes," *CIO Magazine*, April 2007, pp 28-29.

5. Ibid.

6. Michael Hammer and James Champy, *Reengineering the Corporation: A Manifesto for Business Revolution* (New York: HarperBusiness, 1993).

7. American College of Physicians-American Society of Internal Medicine, "Ethics Case Study: Are Health Plan Incentives Hurting Generalist-Specialist Relationships?" *ACP-ASIM Observer*, June 2001, http://www.acponline.org/journals/news/jun01/ethics.htm.

8. Joseph D'Agnese, "Scientific Method Man," *Wired Magazine*, Issue 12.09, September 2004, http://www.wired.com/wired/archive/12.09/rugg.html.

9. Ibid.

10. Ibid.

11. Tom Kelley and Jonathan Littman, *The Ten Faces of Innovation: IDEO's Strategies for Beating the Devil's Advocate & Driving Creativity Throughout Your Organization* (New York: Currency/Doubleday, 2005), pp 7-12.

12. Ibid, p 75.

13. CBC Arts, "Eye Surgeon May Be Needed to Pull Glass from Munch Masterpieces," April 11, 2007, http://www.cbc.ca/arts/artdesign/story/2007/04/11/munch-repairs.html.

14. Jena McGregor, "The Five Faces of the 21st Century Chief," *Business Week*, August 20 & 27, 2007, p 54. (Quoted from James M. Citrin)

15. Buckingham and Coffman, *First, Break All the Rules*.

Chapter 5

1. Peter F. Drucker, *Management: Tasks, Responsibilities, Practices* (New York: Collins, 1993), p 431.

2. Carl H. Builder, Steven C. Bankes, and Richard Nordin, *Command Concepts: A Theory Derived from the Practice of Command and Control* (Washington, DC: RAND Corporation, 1999).

3. Dr. Joanne Sujansky, "Sujansky Says," *KeyGroup Consulting Ezine*, May 2, 2006, http://www.keygroupconsulting. com/ezine5-2-06.php.

4. Ibid.

5. Jack Stack and Bo Burlingham, *The Great Game of Business: Unlocking the Power and Profitability of Open-Book Management* (New York: Doubleday Currency, 2002), p 226.

6. Xenophon, *Xenophon's Cyrus the Great: The Arts of Leadership and War*, ed. Larry Hedrick (New York: St. Martin's Press, 2006), pp 9-10.

Chapter 6

1. Hammer and Champy, *Reengineering the Corporation*.

2. Reprinted by permission of *Harvard Business School Press*. From *Hard Facts, Dangerous Half-Truths, and Total Nonsense: Profiting from Evidence-Based Management* by Jeffrey Pfeffer and Robert I. Sutton. Boston, MA 2006, p 159. Copyright © 2006, by the Harvard Business School Publishing Corporation, all rights reserved.

3. Peter R. Scholtes, *Making Things Happen, Getting Things Done.* New York: McGraw-Hill, 1998, p 127.

4. Dee Hock, "The Art of Chaordic Leadership," in *On Mission and Leadership: A Leader to Leader Guide*, ed. Frances Hesselbein and Rob Johnston (San Francisco: Jossey-Bass, 2002).

5. Builder, Bankes, and Nordin, *Command Concepts*.

6. Hock, "The Art of Chaordic Leadership."

7. Mihaly Csikszentmihalyi, *Good Business: Leadership, Flow, and the Making of Meaning* (New York: Penguin Books, 2004), p 135.

8. Ibid.

9. Buckingham and Coffman, *First, Break All the Rules,* pp 129-132.

10. Reprinted by permission of *Harvard Business School Press.*
From *Hard Facts, Dangerous Half-Truths, and Total Nonsense: Profiting from Evidence-Based Management* by Jeffrey Pfeffer and Robert I. Sutton. Boston, MA 2006, p 150.
Copyright © 2006, by the Harvard Business School Publishing Corporation, all rights reserved.

11. Ibid, p 155.

Chapter 7

1. Csikszentmihalyi, *Good Business,* pp 94-95.

2. Reprinted by permission of *Harvard Business School Press.*
From *What Were They Thinking?: Unconventional Wisdom about Management* by Jeffrey Pfeffer. Boston, MA 2007, p 73.
Copyright © 2007, by the Harvard Business School Publishing Corporation, all rights reserved.

3. Ibid, pp 72-73.

4. Csikszentmihalyi, *Good Business,* p 138.

5. Reprinted by permission of *Harvard Business School Press.*
From *What Were They Thinking?: Unconventional Wisdom about Management* by Jeffrey Pfeffer. Boston, MA 2007, p 39.
Copyright © 2007, by the Harvard Business School Publishing Corporation, all rights reserved.

6. Michelle Conlin, "Smashing the Clock: No Schedules. No Mandatory Meetings. Inside Best Buy's Radical Reshaping of the Workplace." *Business Week Online,* December 11, 2006, http://www.businessweek.com/magazine/content/06_50/b4013001.htm.

7. Ibid.

8. Ibid.

9. Jody Thompson and Cali Ressler, Owners/Cofounders of CultureRx, e-mail communciation with author, September 11, 2007.

10. Ricardo Semler, *Maverick: The Success Story Behind the World's Most Unusual Workplace* (New York: Warner Books, 1995).

11. Lori K. Long, "How to Negotiate a Flexible Work Schedule," *CIO Magazine*, August 29, 2007, http://www.cio.com/article/133800?source=nlt_cioinsider.

12. Semler, *Maverick*, pp 170-172.

13. Matthias Schulz, "Controlled Chaos: European Cities Do Away with Traffic Signs," *Spiegel Online International*, November 16, 2006, http://www.spiegel.de/international/ spiegel/0,1518,448747,00.html.

14. Ibid.

15. Julianne M. Morath and Joanne E. Turnbull, *To Do No Harm: Ensuring Patient Safety in Health Care Organizations* (San Francisco: Jossey-Bass, 2005).

16. Ibid, p 128.

17. Ibid, p 158.

18. Reprinted by permission of *Harvard Business School Press*. From *Hard Facts, Dangerous Half-Truths, and Total Nonsense: Profiting from Evidence-Based Management* by Jeffrey Pfeffer and Robert I. Sutton. Boston, MA 2006, p 200. Copyright © 2006, by the Harvard Business School Publishing Corporation, all rights reserved.

19. Alistair A.R. Cockburn, "Characterizing People as Non-Linear, First-Order Components in Software Development," *HaT Technical Report* 1999.03, October 21, 1999, http://alistair. cockburn.us/index.php/Characterizing_people_as_non-linear,_ first-order_components_in_software_development

20. Ibid.

21. Warren Bennis, *Organizing Genius: The Secrets of Creating Collaboration* (New York: Basic Books, 1997), p 199.

22. Trompenaars, *Did the Pedestrian Die?*, pp 26, 44.

23. Paul Hersey, *The Situational Leader* (Escondido, CA: Center for Leadership Studies, 1984).

24. Csikszentmihalyi, *Good Business*, p 72.

25. U.S. Army, Training and Doctrine Command, *Force XXI Operations: A Concept for the Evolution of Full-Dimensional Operations for the Strategic Army of the Early Twenty-First Century* (Washington, DC: TRADOC Pamphlet 525-5, 1994, 1-5, 3-5), p 124.

26. Bioteams.com, The Bumble Bee: Ken Thompson's Shared Know-How on Team Dynamics, Virtual Collaboration, and Bioteaming, http://www.bioteams.com. (accessed Nov. 20, 2007)

27. Ibid.

Chapter 8

1. Gerald Kreyche, "Appearance vs. Reality: Perception Is More Important Than Reality in Modern Life," *USA Today*, November 1995, http://findarticles.com/p/articles/mi_m1272/is_n2606_v124/ai_17606214.

2. Reprinted by permission of *Harvard Business School Press*. From *Hard Facts, Dangerous Half-Truths, and Total Nonsense: Profiting from Evidence-Based Management* by Jeffrey Pfeffer and Robert I. Sutton. Boston, MA 2006, p 200.
Copyright © 2006, by the Harvard Business School Publishing Corporation, all rights reserved.

3. "Beyond Budget," *PM Network*, September 2006, pp 56-60.

4. Mark Hurst, "Customer Service Is Not Customer Experience," Good Experience, Inc., December 7, 2005, http://www.goodexperience.com/blog/archives/000433.php.

5. Ibid.

6. Trompenaars, *Did the Pedestrian Die?*, p 37.

Chapter 9

1. Semler, *Maverick*, p 132.

2. Ori Brafman and Rod Beckstrom, *The Starfish and the Spider: The Unstoppable Power of Leaderless Organizations* (London: Portfolio Hardcover, 2006), p 35.

3. Ibid, p 32.

4. Ibid, pp 37, 25, 142.

5. Bioteams.com, The Bumblebee. (accessed November 20, 2007)

6. M. Mitchell Waldrop, *Complexity: The Emerging Science at the Edge of Order and Chaos* (New York: Simon and Schuster, 1992), p 241.

7. Ibid, pp 241-242.

8. Ibid, p 279.

9. Ibid, p 280.

10. Margaret Wheatley, *Leadership and the New Science: Discovering Order in a Chaotic World* (San Francisco: Berrett-Koehler, 2006), p 35.

11. Phillip Longman, "The Best Care Anywhere," *Washington Monthly*, January/February 2005, http://www.washingtonmonthly.com/features/2005/0501.longman.html.

12. Ibid.

13. Kenneth W. Kizer, "Health Care, Not Hospitals: Transforming the Veterans' Health Administration," in *Straight from the CEO*, ed. G. William Dauphinais and Colin Price (New York: Fireside, 1998).

14. Anne Laurent, "The Tyranny Of Anecdotes," GovernmentExecutive.com, March 1, 2000, http://www.govexec.com/gpp/0300mr.htm.

15. Trompenaars, *Did the Pedestrian Die?*, p 127.

16. Fons Trompenaars and Charles Hampden-Turner, *21 Leaders for the 21st Century: How Innovative Leaders Manage in the Digital Age* (New York: McGraw-Hill, 2002), p 14.

Chapter 10

1. Joseph L. Badaracco, Jr., *Defining Moments: When Managers Must Choose Between Right and Right* (Boston: Harvard Business School Press, 1997).

2. Jeffrey K. Liker, *The Toyota Way: 14 Management Principles from the World's Greatest Manufacturer* (New York: McGraw-Hill, 2004), pp 37-40.

3. Jason Notte, "Grinding out a Living: Ethopian Farmers Battle Starbucks for a Better Marketplace." *Metro*, March 26, 2007.

4. Stephanie Overby, "Order-Takers to Innovators: Four CIO 100 Honorees Share Their Steps for Making the Change." *CIO Magazine*, August 15, 2007, p 50.

5. Dwyer, *The Shifting Sources of Power and Influence*, p 37.

6. Csikszentmihalyi, *Good Business*, p 36.

7. Semler, *Maverick*, p 130.

8. Semler, *Maverick*.

9. Michael Orey, "Bittersweet Memories at Hershey," *Business Week*, October 15, 2007, p 12.

10. Badaracco, *Defining Moments*, pp 6-7.

11. Dobrin, *Ethics for Everyone*.

12. M. Neil Browne and Stuart M. Keeley, *Asking the Right Questions: A Guide to Critical Thinking* (Upper Saddle River, NJ: Pearson Education, 2004).

13. Badaracco, *Defining Moments*.

14. Syque, "Socratic Questions," ChangingMinds.org, http://www.changingminds.org/techniques/questioning/socratic_questions.htm.

    Note: Questions adapted from *The Art of Socratic Questioning*, by Richard Paul and Linda Elder (Dillon Beach, CA: Foundation for Critical Thinking, 2006)

15. Peter M. Senge, *The Fifth Discipline: The Art & Practice of the Learning Organization, 1st Edition* (New York: Doubleday/Currency, 1990)

16. Wheatley, *Leadership and the New Science*, p 10.

17. Wheatley, *Leadership and the New Science*.

18. Trompenaars and Hampden-Turner, *21 Leaders for the 21st Century*, p 15.

19. Scholtes, *The Leader's Handbook*, p 38.

20. Hammer and Champy, *Reengineering the Corporation*, p 8.

21. Scholtes, *The Leader's Handbook*, p 394.

22. Jeffrey Pfeffer and Robert I. Sutton, "Five Principles of EBM," Evidence-Based Management, http://www.evidence-basedmanagement.com. (accessed November 20, 2007)

23. Fred Hapgood "Making Connections," *CIO Magazine*, October 1, 2007, pp 71-72.

24. Reprinted by permission of *Harvard Business School Press*. From *Hard Facts, Dangerous Half-Truths, and Total Nonsense: Profiting from Evidence-Based Management* by Jeffrey Pfeffer and Robert I. Sutton. Boston, MA 2006, p 162.
   Copyright © 2006, by the Harvard Business School Publishing Corporation, all rights reserved.
   Note: Referencing a Robbins-Gioia survey of 232 IT executives.

25. Stephanie Quappe and Giovanna Cantatore, "What Is Cultural Awareness Anyway? How Do I Build It?" Culturosity.com, July 22, 2006, http://www.culturosity.com/articles/whatisculturalawareness.htm.

26. "Intelligence in Men and Women Is a Gray and White Matter," *ScienceDaily*, January 22, 2005, http://www.sciencedaily.com/releases/2005/01/050121100142.htm.

27. Ibid.

28. James T. Hardee, MD, "An Overview of Empathy," *The Permanente Journal, A Focus on Patient-Centered Care and Office Practice Management:* Vol. 7, No. 4, Fall 2003, http://xnet.kp.org/permanentejournal/fall03/cpc.html.

29. Tom Coens and Mary Jenkins, *Abolishing Performance Appraisals: Why They Backfire and What to Do Instead* (San Francisco: Berrett-Koehler, 2002), pp 148-150.

30. Ibid, p 171.

Bibliography

Allen, David. *Getting Things Done: The Art of Stress-Free Productivity.* New York: Penguin, 2001.

American College of Physicians-American Society of Internal Medicine. "Ethics Case Study: Are Health Plan Incentives Hurting Generalist-Specialist Relationships?" *ACP-ASIM Observer,* June 2001, http://www.acponline.org/journals/news/jun01/ethics.htm.

Arnauld, Antoine. *The Art of Thinking: Port-Royal Logic.* Translated by James Dickoff and Patricia James. Indianapolis, IN: The Bobbs-Merrill Company, 1964.

Badaracco, Joseph L., Jr. *Defining Moments: When Managers Must Choose between Right and Right.* Boston: Harvard Business School Press, 1997.

Bennett, Drake. "Best Practices: Unlike the Army's Walter Reed Hospital, the VA Hospital System Is Ranked, by Many Measures, as the Best in the Country." *The Boston Globe,* March 11, 2007, http://www.boston.com/news/globe/ideas/articles/2007/03/11/best_practices/.

Bennis, Warren. *Organizing Genius: The Secrets of Creating Collaboration.* New York: Basic Books, 1997.

"Beyond Budget." *PM Network,* September 2006.

Bilanich, Bud. *Fixing Performance Problems: Common Sense Ideas That Work.* Charleston, SC: BookSurge Publishing, 2005.

Bioteams.com. The Bumble Bee: Ken Thompson's Shared Know-How on Team Dynamics, Virtual Collaboration, and Bioteaming, http://www.bioteams.com.

Blackburn, Simon. *Being Good: An Introduction to Ethics.* Oxford: Oxford University Press, 2001.

Blanchard, Ken. *Leading at a Higher Level: Blanchard on Leadership and Creating High Performance Organizations.* Upper Saddle River, NJ: Prentice Hall, 2006.

Brafman, Ori, and Rod Beckstrom. *The Starfish and the Spider: The Unstoppable Power of Leaderless Organizations.* London: Portfolio Hardcover, 2006.

Browne, M. Neil, and Stuart M. Keeley. *Asking the Right Questions: A Guide to Critical Thinking.* Upper Saddle River, NJ: Pearson Education, 2004.

Buckingham, Marcus. *The One Thing You Need to Know: ...About Great Managing, Great Leading, and Sustained Individual Success.* New York: Free Press, 2005.

Buckingham, Marcus, and Donald O. Clifton. *Now, Discover Your Strengths.* New York: Free Press, 2001.

Buckingham, Marcus, and Curt Coffman. *First, Break All the Rules: What the World's Greatest Managers Do Differently.* New York: Simon & Schuster, 1999.

Builder, Carl H., Steven C. Bankes, and Richard Nordin. *Command Concepts: A Theory Derived from the Practice of Command and Control.* Washington, DC: RAND Corporation, 1999.

Charan, Ram. "Five Rules for Setting the Right Priorities." Yahoo! Finance, April 11, 2007, http://finance.yahoo.com/expert/article/companyknow/29003.

Cockburn, Alistair A.R. "Characterizing People as Non-Linear, First-Order Components in Software Development." *HaT Technical Report 1999.03*, October 21, 1999, http://alistair.cockburn.us/index.php/Characterizing_people_as_non-linear,_first-order_components_in_software_development.

Coens, Tom, and Mary Jenkins. *Abolishing Performance Appraisals: Why They Backfire and What to Do Instead.* San Francisco: Berrett-Koehler, 2002.

Collins, Jim, and Jerry I. Porras. *Built to Last: Successful Habits of Visionary Companies.* New York: Collins, 2002.

Conlin, Michelle. "Smashing the Clock: No Schedules. No Mandatory Meetings. Inside Best Buy's Radical Reshaping of the Workplace." *Business Week Online*, December 11, 2006, http://www.businessweek.com/magazine/content/06_50/b4013001.htm.

Covey, Stephen R. *Principle-Centered Leadership*. New York: Simon & Schuster, 1991.

Coyote, Carmine. "Seeing in Black and White." Slow Leadership, August 16, 2006, http://www.slowleadership.org/2006/08/seeing-in-black-and-white.html.

Crandall, N. Frederic, and Marc J. Wallace, Jr. *Work & Rewards in the Virtual Workplace*. New York: AMACOM, 1998.

Critical Thinking. Wikepedia, http://en.wikipedia.org/wiki/Critical_Thinking.

Csikszentmihalyi, Mihaly. *Good Business: Leadership, Flow, and the Making of Meaning*. New York: Penguin Books, 2004.

Cusumano, Michael A., and Kentarảo Nobeoka. *Thinking Beyond Lean: How Multi-Project Management Is Transforming Product Development at Toyota and Other Companies*. New York: Free Press, 1998.

D'Agnese, Joseph. "Scientific Method Man." *Wired Magazine*, Issue 12.09, September 2004, http://www.wired.com/wired/archive/12.09/rugg.html.

DeCarlo, Douglas. *Extreme Project Management: Using Leadership, Principles, and Tools to Deliver Value in the Face of Volatility*. San Francisco: Jossey-Bass, 2004.

Depression Learning Path. All or Nothing Thinking. Uncommon Knowledge, Ltd, http://www.clinical-depression.co.uk/Understanding_Depression/all_nothing.htm.

Dobrin, Arthur. *Ethics for Everyone: How to Increase Your Moral Intelligence*. New York: J. Wiley & Sons, 2002.

Drucker, Peter F. *Management: Tasks, Responsibilities, Practices*. New York: Collins, 1993.

Drucker, Peter F., and Joseph A. Maciariello. *The Effective Executive in Action: A Journal for Getting the Right Things Done*. New York: Collins, 2006.

Dwyer, Charles. *The Shifting Sources of Power and Influence*. Tampa, FL: American College of Physician Executives, 1991.

Eckman, Paul. *Emotions Revealed: Recognizing Faces and Feelings to Improve Communication and Emotional Life.* New York: Owl Books, 2003.

"Eye Surgeon May Be Needed to Pull Glass from Munch Masterpieces." CBC Arts, April 11, 2007, http://www.cbc.ca/arts/artdesign/story/2007/04/11/munch-repairs.html.

Fournies, Ferdinand F. *Why Employees Don't Do What They're Supposed to Do and What to Do About It.* New York: McGraw-Hill, 1999.

Franklin, Benjamin, *The Autobiography of Benjamin Franklin.* Leonard W. Labaree, Ralph L. Ketcham, Helen C. Boatfield, and Helene H. Fineman, eds. New Haven, CT: Yale University Press, 2003.

Gladwell, Malcolm. *Blink: The Power of Thinking without Thinking.* New York: Little, Brown and Co., 2005.

Glaser, Judith E. *Creating We: Change I-Thinking to WE-Thinking & Build a Healthy, Thriving Organization.* Cincinnati, OH: Adams Media Corporation, 2005.

―――. *The DNA of Leadership: Leverage Your Instincts to Communicate, Differentiate, Innovate.* Avon, MA: Platinum Press, 2006.

Goleman, Daniel. *Emotional Intelligence.* New York: Bantam Books, 1995.

―――. *Social Intelligence: The New Science of Human Relationships.* New York: Bantam Books, 2006.

Grinder, Michael. *The Elusive Obvious: The Science of Non-Verbal Communication.* Battle Ground, WA: Michael Grinder & Associates, 2007.

Hammer, Michael. "The Process Audit: A New Framework. As Comprehensive as It Is Easy to Apply, Is Helping Companies Plan and Execute Process-Based Transformations." *Harvard Business Review,* 2007.

Hammer, Michael, and James Champy. *Reengineering the Corporation: A Manifesto for Business Revolution.* New York: HarperBusiness, 1993.

Hammond, John S., Ralph L. Keeney, and Howard Raiffa. "Even Swaps: A Rational Method for Making Tradeoffs." In *Harvard Business Review on Decision Making*. Boston: Harvard Business School Pub., 2001.

Hammond, Sue Annis. *The Thin Book of Appreciative Inquiry*. Bend, OR: Thin Book Publishing, 1998.

Hapgood, Fred. "Making Connections." *CIO Magazine*, October 1, 2007.

Hardee, James T. "An Overview of Empathy." *The Permanente Journal*, http://xnet.kp.org/permanentejournal/fall03/cpc.html.

Heineman, Ben W. "Integrity Land Mines: An Inside Look at How GE Has Worked to Build a Culture That Sustains Both High Performance and High Integrity." *Harvard Business Review*, 2007.

Hersey, Paul. *The Situational Leader*. Escondido, CA: Center for Leadership Studies, 1984.

Hock, Dee. "The Art of Chaordic Leadership" In *On Mission and Leadership: A Leader to Leader Guide*. Frances Hesselbein and Rob Johnston, eds. San Francisco: Jossey-Bass, 2002.

Hurst, Mark. "Customer Service Is Not Customer Experience." Goodexperience.com, December 7, 2005, http://www.goodexperience.com/blog/archives/000433.php.

Iaccoca, Lee. *Where Have All the Leaders Gone?* New York: Scribner, 2007.

"Intelligence in Men and Women Is a Gray and White Matter" *Science Daily*, January 22, 2005, http://www.sciencedaily.com/releases/2005/01/050121100142.htm.

Johnson, M. Eric. "Put People Before Processes." *CIO Magazine*, April 2007.

Kelley, Tom, and Jonathan Littman. *The Ten Faces of Innovation: IDEO's Strategies for Beating the Devil's Advocate & Driving Creativity Throughout Your Organization*. New York: Currency/Doubleday, 2005.

Kizer, Kenneth W. "Health Care, Not Hospitals: Transforming the Veterans' Health Administration" in *Straight from the CEO*. G. William Dauphinais and Colin Price, eds. New York: Fireside, 1998.

Kozak-Holland, Mark. *Avoiding Project Disaster: Titanic Lessons for IT Executives*. Ontario, Canada: Multi-Media Publications, 2006.

Kreyche, Gerald. "Appearance vs. Reality: Perception Is More Important Than Reality in Modern Life." *USA Today*, November 1995, http://findarticles. com/p/articles/mi_m1272/is_n2606_v124/ai_17606214.

Kushel, Gerald. *Reaching the Peak Performance Zone: How to Motivate Yourself and Others to Excel*. New York: AMACOM, 1994.

Laurent, Anne. "The Tyranny Of Anecdotes," GovernmentExecutive. com, March 1, 2000, http://www.govexec.com/gpp/0300mr. htm.

Lencioni, Patrick. *Silos, Politics, and Turf Wars: A Leadership Fable About Destroying the Barriers That Turn Colleagues into Competitors*. San Francisco: Jossey-Bass, 2006.

Liker, Jeffrey K. *The Toyota Way: 14 Management Principles from the World's Greatest Manufacturer*. New York: McGraw-Hill, 2004.

Littky, Dennis, and Samantha Grabelle. *The Big Picture: Education Is Everyone's Business*. Alexandria, VA: Association for Supervision and Curriculum Development, 2004.

Long, Lori K. "How to Negotiate a Flexible Work Schedule." *CIO Magazine*. August 29, 2007. http://www.cio. com/article/133800?source=nlt_cioinsider.

Longman, Phillip. "The Best Care Anywhere" *Washington Monthly*, January/February 2005, http://www.washingtonmonthly. com/features/2005/0501.longman.html.

Ludema, James D., Diana Whitney, Bernard J. Mohr, and Thomas J. Griffin. *The Appreciative Inquiry Summit: A Practitioner's Guide for Leading Large-Group Change*. San Francisco: Berrett-Koehler, 2003.

Machiavelli, Niccolò. *The Prince*. New York: Bantam Classics, 1984.

Maimonides, Moses, Julius Guttman, and Daniel H. Frank. *The Guide of the Perplexed*. Translated by Chaim Rabin. Indianapolis, IN: Hackett Publishing Company, 1995.

Manas, Jerry. *Napoleon on Project Management: Timeless Lessons in Planning, Execution, and Leadership*. Nashville: Thomas Nelson, 2006.

Maxwell, John C. *The 360 Degree Leader: Developing Your Influence from Anywhere in the Organization*. Nashville: Thomas Nelson, 2006.

Mazhar, Uzma. "Black & White Thinking," 2005, http://www.crescentlife.com/evolving%20self/black&whitethinking.htm.

McGregor, Jena. "The Five Faces of the 21st Century Chief." *Business Week*, August 20 & 27, 2007.

Merron, Keith. *Consulting Mastery: How the Best Make the Biggest Difference*. San Francisco: Berrett-Koehler Publishers, 2005.

Monk, Linda R. *The Words We Live By: Your Annotated Guide to the Constitution*, 1st Edition. New York: Hyperion, 2003.

Morath, Julianne M., and Joanne E. Turnbull. *To Do No Harm: Ensuring Patient Safety in Health Care Organizations*. San Francisco: Jossey-Bass, 2005.

Musashi, Miyamoto, and Stephen F. Kaufman. *The Martial Artist's Book of Five Rings*. North Clarendon, VT: Turtle Publishing, 1994.

Nawash, Kamal. "A Moderate Muslim View of Islamic Terrorism," http://www.crescentlife.com/heal%20the%20world/moderate_muslim_view_of_islamic_terrorism.htm.

Newman, David. *Unconsulting: 95 Ways to Get More Done, Make More Money, and Rediscover the Joy of Business*. Foster City, CA: Cafe Press, 2004.

Nickols, Fred. "Generalist or Specialist: Which Do I Consult?" Distance Consulting, 2003, http://www.nickols.us/.

———. "Generalists and Specialists: Unraveling the Mystery." Distance Consulting, 2004, http://www.nickols.us/.

———. "Skullworks: Articles by Fred Nickols." http://www.nickols.us/.

Notte, Jason. "Grinding out a Living: Ethopian Farmers Battle Starbucks for a Better Marketplace." *Metro*, March 26, 2007.

Orey, Michael. "Bittersweet Memories at Hershey." *Business Week*, October 15, 2007.

Overby, Stephanie. "Order-Takers to Innovators: Four CIO 100 Honorees Share Their Steps for Making the Change." *CIO Magazine*, August 15, 2007.

Pfeffer, Jeffrey. *What Were They Thinking? Unconventional Wisdom About Management.* Boston: Harvard Business School Press, 2007.

Pfeffer, Jeffrey, and Robert I. Sutton, "Five Principles of EBM," Evidence-Based Management, http://www.evidence-basedmanagement.com.

———. *Hard Facts, Dangerous Half-Truths, and Total Nonsense: Profiting from Evidence-Based Management.* Boston: Harvard Business School Press, 2006.

Pink, Daniel H. *A Whole New Mind: Moving from the Information Age to the Conceptual Age.* New York: Riverhead Books, 2005.

Plato. *Plato: Apology.* James J. Helm, ed. Wauconda, Illinois: Bolchazy-Carducci Publishers, 1997.

Porter, Michael. *Redefining Health Care: Creating Value-Based Competition on Results.* Boston: Harvard Business School Press, 2006.

Quappe, Stephanie, and Giovanna Cantatore, "What Is Cultural Awareness Anyway? How Do I Build it?" Culturosity.com, July 22, 2006, http://www.culturosity.com/articles/whatisculturalawareness.htm.

Rath, Tom, and Donald O. Clifton. *How Full Is Your Bucket?: Positive Strategies for Work and Life.* New York: Gallup Press, 2004.

Richards, Chet. *Certain to Win: The Strategy of John Boyd, Applied to Business.* Philadelphia, PA: Xlibris, 2004.

Rosenbluth, Hal F., and Diane McFerrin Peters. *The Customer Comes Second: Put Your People First and Watch 'Em Kick Butt.* New York: Harper Business, 2002.

Rosenzweig, Phil. *The Halo Effect... And the Eight Other Business Delusions That Deceive Managers.* New York: Free Press, 2007.

Russell, Bill, and David Falkner. *Russell Rules: 11 Lessons on Leadership From the Twentieth Century's Greatest Winner.* New York: NAL Trade, 2002.

Sample, Ruth J., Charles W. Mills, and James P. Sterba, eds. *Philosophy: The Big Questions.* Oxford, UK: Blackwell Publishing, Ltd, 2004.

Scholtes, Peter R. *The Leader's Handbook: Making Things Happen, Getting Things Done.* New York: McGraw-Hill, 1998.

Schultz, Howard, and Dori Jones Yang. *Pour Your Heart into It: How Starbucks Built a Company One Cup at a Time.* New York: Hyperion, 1997.

Schulz, Matthias "Controlled Chaos: European Cities Do Away with Traffic Signs." *Spiegel Online International,* November 16, 2006, http://www.spiegel.de/international/ spiegel/0,1518,448747,00.html.

Semler, Ricardo. *Maverick: The Success Story Behind the World's Most Unusual Workplace.* New York: Warner Books, 1995.

———. *The Seven-Day Weekend: Changing the Way Work Works.* New York: Portfolio, 2004.

Senge, Peter M. *The Fifth Discipline: The Art & Practice of the Learning Organization,* 1st Edition. New York: Doubleday/Currency, 1990.

"Socratic Questions." Syque. ChangingMinds.org, http:// changingminds.org/techniques/questioning/socratic_ questions.htm.

Spitzer, Dean R. *Transforming Performance Measurement: Rethinking the Way We Measure and Drive Organizational Success.* New York: AMACOM, 2007.

Stack, Jack, and Bo Burlingham. *The Great Game of Business: Unlocking the Power and Profitability of Open-Book Management.* New York: Doubleday Currency, 2002.

———. *A Stake in the Outcome: Building a Culture of Ownership for the Long-Term Success of Your Business.* New York: Doubleday Currency, 2002.

Stringer, Hank, and Rusty Rueff. *Talent Force: A New Manifesto for the Human Side of Business.* Upper Saddle River, NJ: Pearson/ Prentice Hall, 2006.

Sujansky, Dr. Joanne. "Sujansky Says." *KeyGroup Consulting Ezine,* May 2, 2006, http://www.keygroupconsulting. com/ezine5-2-06.php.

Surowiecki, James. *The Wisdom of Crowds.* New York: Anchor Books, 2005.

Tapscott, Don, and Anthony D. Williams. *Wikinomics: How Mass Collaboration Changes Everything.* New York: Portfolio, 2006.

"Testing Firms Left Behind: "No Child" Demands Push Some Companies to the Limit." Associated Press. *Metro,* March 26, 2007.

Thompson, Bruce. "Black & White Thinking." Cuyamaca College, http://www.cuyamaca.edu/brucethompson/Fallacies/ black&white.asp.

———. "Fallacy Page." Cuyamaca College, http://www.cuyamaca. edu/brucethompson/Fallacies/intro_fallacies.asp.

Trompenaars, Fons. *Did the Pedestrian Die? Insights from the World's Greatest Culture Guru.* Oxford: Capstone Publishing Limited, 2003.

Trompenaars, Fons and Charles Hampden-Turner. *21 Leaders for the 21st Century: How Innovative Leaders Manage in the Digital Age.* New York: McGraw-Hill, 2002.

Tsouras, Peter G., ed. *The Greenhill Dictionary of Military Quotations.* London: Greenhill Books, 2000.

U.S. Army, Training and Doctrine Command, *Force XXI Operations: A Concept for the Evolution of Full-Dimensional Operations for the Strategic Army of the Early Twenty-First Century* (Washington, DC: TRADOC Pamphlet 525-5, 1994, 1-5, 3-5).

"Virtuous Circles and Vicious Circles." Wikipedia, http:// en.wikipedia.org/wiki/Virtuous_circle_and_vicious_circle.

Waldrop, M. Mitchell. *Complexity: The Emerging Science at the Edge of Order and Chaos.* New York: Simon and Schuster, 1992.

Wheatley, Margaret. *Leadership and the New Science: Discovering Order in a Chaotic World.* San Francisco: Berrett-Koehler, 2006.

Williams, Byron. "Black and White Thinking Doesn't Work in a Gray World." *The Huffington Post,* October 2, 2006, http://www.huffingtonpost.com/byron-williams/black-and-white-thinking-_b_30747.html.

Xenophon. *Xenophon's Cyrus the Great: The Arts of Leadership and War.* Larry Hedrick, ed. New York: St. Martin's Press, 2006.

Yourdon, Edward. *Death March: The Complete Software Developer's Guide to Surviving "Mission Impossible" Projects, Yourdon Press Computing Series.* Upper Saddle River, NJ: Prentice Hall PTR, 1999.

Zimbardo, Philip G. "How We Become Like the Enemy." http://www.crescentlife.com/heal%20the%20world/how_we_become_like_the_enemy.htm.

———. *The Lucifer Effect: Understanding How Good People Turn Evil.* New York: Random House, 2007.

About the Author

Jerry Manas is the author of the international bestseller, *Napoleon on Project Management* (Nelson Business, April 2006) and cofounder of PMThink! (www.pmthink.com), a popular leadership and project management blog site. An organizational architect with a specialty in project management and virtual team dynamics, he is passionate about helping leaders create flexible, yet integrated, organizations and teams.

His work has been cited by management guru Tom Peters and highlighted in a variety of publications, including *Leadership Excellence, The National Post, The Globe and Mail, The Chicago Sun Times*, and *The Houston Chronicle*. He has written numerous articles and appeared on radio programs nationwide with the release of his first book, which *Kirkus Reviews* called, "The ultimate case study in effective project management."

Through his consulting company, The Marengo Group, Jerry works with partners and clients to facilitate the implementation of the ideas and principles outlined in his books. His Service-Oriented Project Management (SOPM) framework, built around these principles, has been recognized as an innovative achievement model that fosters systems thinking and a client-focused mindset.

With an endless curiosity, a passion for research, and a deep interest in multiple disciplines, including history, science, philosophy, and more, Jerry often writes on lessons gained from unexpected places and frequently speaks on the topic to business leaders and university students.

Jerry resides in Philadelphia, Pennsylvania, with his wife Sharon and daughter Elizabeth. You can contact Jerry at jerry.manas@gmail.com, or visit his Web site, www.manasbooks.com, which includes information on Jerry's teleconsulting services, useful articles, blogs, podcasts, and more.

Acknowledgments

I could not have written this book without the help and support of others. Once again, my wife Sharon was a great source of support, not only putting up with the book as "the other woman" (as she called it), but listening to me expound endlessly about new ideas and theories. My daughter Elizabeth, now six, gives me endless inspiration to try to make the world a better place for future generations.

I'd like to thank my agent, Daniel Bial, who is always there for me with his expert guidance and insights about the publishing industry.

Mary Lofsness, my editor at RMC Publications, was a pillar of strength throughout the development of this book, challenging me to clarify points and think through ideas, and always there when I needed objective advice. Along with Mary, I offer a special thanks to Laurie Diethelm and Jess Snively, also of RMC's Editorial Department, whose graphic design talents and commitment to excellence made such a difference. I must thank those at RMC who believed in the idea for this book and enabled it to happen, such as Marketing Director Eric Rudolf, Vice President and Legal Counsel Tim Mulcahy, and, of course, the Founder and CEO of RMC, Rita Mulcahy, whose books and products I relied on to achieve my Project Management Professional certification those many years ago. It is RMC's dedication to offering learners an "ecosystem" of support, in the form of online and classroom-based courses, training materials, and other ancillary products that enticed me to sign with them, and I'm glad I did.

As for my own "ecosystem," I must thank my parents Sid and Barbara, for their endless support and encouragement; my brother Eric (who, as he did with my last book, made sure my scientific explanations weren't science-fiction); my in-laws Norman and Sallie Olson (Norman, a former psychologist and human factors expert, was, as always, a wealth of information); and my extended family: Denise Manas, Joe and Heather Olson, Rise Harris, Mitchell Harris, and, of course, the next generation: my nieces Aubrey and Gillian Manas and my nephew Alex Olson.

Many thanks to Jerome Jewell, who opened my eyes to topics such as asking the right questions, setting the right priorities, systems thinking, and emotional intelligence. If it weren't for my inspiring conversations with Jerome, which also led to our seminar, this book would not exist. I must also, of course, thank the attendees at the Leadership Quadrant seminar, whose contributions led to the seminar's outcomes.

I'd like to extend a special thanks to Judith E. Glaser, not only for writing the wonderful foreword for this book, but for her guidance and support as well. Judith opened my eyes to many new topics, such as Appreciative Inquiry, neuro-linguistic programming, the impact of genetic research on human achievement, and more. I was honored to be included in Judith's First International Creating We Summit this year, where I had the fortunate experience of connecting on a deep level with an amazing, cross-disciplinary group of thought leaders from all over the world. Our team truly bonded, and there will be much to come from our collaboration.

I must acknowledge the summit participants, whose insights served as validation for much of the material in this book and inspiration for books to come: Rex Jung, Jo Washington, Nancy Ring, Peg Aldridge, Katinka Nicou, Louise van Rhyn, Kate Grace MacElveen, Bob Fuller, Stan Labovitz, Charles Jones, Coley Bailey, Deborah Hicks Madanek, Catherine Mullally, Liz Franklin, Deborah Dumaine, Richard Glaser, Jan Goldstoff, Lisa Giruzzi, Pat Tyre, Jane Hewson, Lara Herscovitch, Fernando Natalici, and last, but certainly not least, Brian Penry, whose brilliant ideas, insights, and consulting on branding and design have been invaluable. I'd like to add an additional thanks to summit attendee Rex Jung, for allowing me to reference his groundbreaking research on the human brain. (Dr. Jung has recently been awarded a $600,000 grant from the John Templeton Foundation to study the roots of creativity in the brain).

224

I thank Cali Ressler and Jody Thompson, from CultureRx, for taking time out of their busy schedules to address my questions on their Results-Only Work Environment (ROWE) model, which they implemented at Best Buy. I also thank Claude Emond, a kindred spirit and fellow believer in finding lessons from strange places. Claude's exhaustive review of the draft, along with his insightful comments and sage advice, made a huge impact on the final version of this book.

There are others with whom I've had numerous discussions who have had a great influence on this book. Among them are my PMThink! friends and colleagues, Frank Miller (our Starbucks brainstorming sessions are forever inspiring), Graham McHardy (who always has unique insights I can use), and Garry Booker (whose pioneering viewpoints never cease to amaze me). Additional sources of inspiration are Bill Sohl (I told him I'd acknowledge our many intriguing lunchtime conversations, but he didn't believe me); Yuriy Belodray and Rafael Sharafutdinov, from Ukraine (our e-mails got me thinking about complexity theory); Ken Thompson (whose pioneering work on biological teams got me thinking in new directions); and Doug DeCarlo, creator of eXtreme Project Management (who first introduced me to the quantum versus Newtonian mindset).

Others I'd like to acknowledge are Bud Bilanich, for his general support and for letting me include his eleven reasons for poor performance; Todd Colbeck, for his insights on strength-based leadership and his guidance for our joint-Webinars; Cornelius Fitchner, Dina Scott, Matt Scheaff, and Shawn Futterer, for their encouragement and camaraderie in the project management world; and Gaelen O'Connell from Mindjet, for her ongoing support and for hosting my Webinars. (I'm a big believer in their *MindManager* software for brainstorming, mapping ideas, facilitating meetings, managing projects, and more, but I digress.) Once again, I thank Lori Lisi, my publicist/proposal editor, and Brian Dimeo, whose artistic creativity never ceases to amaze me. (Brian designed the Marengo Group logo based on my very strange request to integrate a horse, a chess piece, and an hourglass; for the full story, see my Web site).

I must thank Ruth Rogers, for her ongoing friendship and our many philosophical discussions. And I cannot forget my other good friends, Bill Talley, Maggie Mullen, Peter and Jan Pacitti, David Petty, Nikki Lang, Tom Iobst, Tracy Lango, Randall Goodman, Barry Rosenblatt, Joe Beletz, Larry Ketzes, Scott Talis, Ron Singer, Billy Love, Glenn Cantor, Eric Schlanger, Rich Newman, Todd Handler, Rich Teplitsky, Eric Cantor, and Joe Farrell. I'd also like to thank Linda Dubrow-Marshall for her always-helpful insights.

I must acknowledge those with whom I've worked recently at The Children's Hospital of Philadelphia (CHOP). Voted the number one children's hospital year after year, it's an honor to contribute to an organization with such a worthy mission. While to name all of the wonderful people I've worked with there would fill another page, I'd particularly like to thank Diane Stanton for her support and for allowing me the opportunity to help make a difference.

Finally, I'd like to thank those whose work came before mine, and whose exhaustive research and groundbreaking ideas enabled me to benefit from their insights. These are true thought leaders, such as Fons Trompenaars and Charles Hampden-Turner (whose concepts on reconciling, as opposed to balancing, multiple truths were a great inspiration), Jeff Pfeffer and Bob Sutton (whose insights on evidence-based management really opened my eyes), Charles Dwyer (whose speech on people's "real" value systems allowed me to see things from new perspectives), Marcus Buckingham and Curt Coffman (whose uncommon wisdom changed my views on leadership), Dennis Littky (whose thoughts regarding school reforms apply equally to business), Ricardo Semler (whose methods at Semco show that there is a better way), and Tom Peters (whose work always inspires me to challenge the status quo).

To all of those listed, and to those I may have inadvertently omitted, I thank you.